THE
MAGIC
LADDER
TO
SUCCESS

THE
MAGIC
LADDER
TO
SUCCESS

NAPOLEON HILL

Published 2022 by Gildan Media LLC
aka G&D Media
www.GandDmedia.com

THE MAGIC LADDER TO SUCCESS. Introduction copyright ©2022 by
Mitch Horowitz. Originally published in 1930. All rights reserved.

Front Cover design by David Rheinhardt of Pyrographx

Interior design by Meghan Day Healey of Story Horse, LLC

Library of Congress Cataloging-in-Publication Data is available
upon request

ISBN: 978-1-7225-0235-5

10   9   8   7   6   5   4   3   2   1

———•••———

THIS BOOK IS AFFECTIONATELY DEDICATED TO THAT GREAT ARMY OF UNSEEN STUDENTS AND FRIENDS OF THE AUTHOR'S, THROUGHOUT THE WORLD, WHO HAVE FOUND THEIR PLACES IN THE WORLD'S WORK THROUGH THE LAW OF SUCCESS PHILOSOPHY WHICH IS BRIEFLY PRESENTED IN THESE PAGES. THE AUTHOR WISHES ESPECIALLY TO EXPRESS HERE HIS THANKS TO THOSE FAITHFUL STUDENTS WHO OFFERED HIM ENCOURAGEMENT DURING THE YEARS OF POVERTY AND STRUGGLE THROUGH WHICH HE HAD TO PASS WHILE THE LAW OF SUCCESS PHILOSOPHY WAS IN THE MAKING. FINALLY, THE AUTHOR WISHES TO PAY TRIBUTE TO ALL WHO, DURING HIS LEAN YEARS, TRIED TO DESTROY HIM WITH RIDICULE AND TO HIS ENEMIES WHO RESORTED TO MORE VIOLENT METHODS, FOR THEY ARMED HIM WITH THE DETERMINATION AND THE PERSISTENCE TO SEE HIS LABORS COMPLETED.

———•••———

Original Edition Note

This book presents, in a greatly condensed form, the entire seventeen factors out of which the Law of Success philosophy was evolved. This philosophy represents all that the most successful men who ever lived have learned about the achievement of success in practically every sort of human endeavor. Its compilation has cost a fortune, to say nothing of the better part of a lifetime of effort upon the part of the author.

Contents

LESSON ONE The Master Mind   35

The eight basic motivating forces which underlie all human action. The relationship between sexual urge and genius. The value of transmutation of sex energy. *The ten major sources of mind stimulation.* *Power*—what it is and how to organize and use it. *Co-operation*—the psychology of co-operative effort. *Henry Ford, Thomas A. Edison,* and *Harvey Firestone*—how they acquired power through the Master Mind principle. *The big six*—how they made the Master Mind principle yield them more than $25,000,000 a year.

How to stimulate the imaginative faculty. *Telepathy*—how thought vibrations pass from one mind to another, through the agency of the ether. How salesmen and public speakers may "tune in" on the thoughts of their audiences. *Vibration*—described by Dr. Alexander Graham Bell, inventor of the long distance telephone.

Air and *ether*—how they carry vibrations. How and why ideas flash into the mind. *Andrew Carnegie* responsible for organization of Law of Success. *Elbert H. Gary* approves the Law of Success philosophy. *One million dollars* earned by students of Law of Success.

Spiritualism—what it is and how it works. Why some people antagonize others at sight, without knowing it. Why *Henry Ford* is the most powerful man living.

What we have learned from "Nature's Bible." *Chemistry of the mind*—how it will make or destroy you. What is meant by the *Psychological moment* in salesmanship.

The mind becomes devitalized—how to "recharge" it. The value and meaning of *harmony* in all co-operative efforts. Of what does *Henry Ford's* assets consist? The answer.

Education—what it is and what it *is not!* The secret of all financial success, as gathered from the study of 100 successful men and 20,000 failures. The relationship between vibration (or energy) and matter.

Introduction

∽

Hill's Most Essential Principles
of Living in a Nutshell
by Mitch Horowitz

This book began in the mind of one of Napoleon Hill's students. After the 1928 publication of Hill's sixteen-volume *Law of Success*, the writer made a practice of holding "interviews," or what we today would call creativity sessions, with individual students.

One student proved particularly insightful. "Within fifteen minutes after her arrival at the author's office," he wrote, "she had 'stepped up' the vibrations of her mind to where she was 'tuning in' on the Master Mind principles." As a result, Hill continued, a wave of ideas began to "flash" into the student's mind. He wrote down forty of them, the first of which was: "Rewrite the Law of Success philosophy in a brief form which can be presented in one volume, at a very low cost, so it can be placed in the hands of hundreds of thousands of students who might otherwise never have the benefit of such a philosophy of success." Hill's *Magic Ladder to Success*, published in 1930, became that volume.

This Original Classic Edition is a working guide to Hill's broadest range of ideas. One of the benefits of *The Magic Ladder to Success* is that Hill writes boldly on his theory of how to use "sex energy" as a force for creativity and success. In all of his books, Hill makes the sometimes enigmatic point that the sexual urge is, in fact, the sensation of life's creative force flowing through the individual, and that if this urge, while still being respected on its physical terms, can be channeled *in the direction of achievement*, it may result in works of excellence and even genius. In brief, this technique requires *substituting* another aim or desire for the object of one's sexual urge—and then allowing your creative energies to channel in that direction. Again, Hill does not mean stifling or denying physical sexuality. Not at all. In fact, he underscores the therapeutic value of sexual contact. But rather, Hill induces the reader to become a kind of alchemist who understands redirecting intimate forces for both mental and outer ends.

Hill shrewdly notes that the motive of sexual expression is perhaps the strongest of all motives, since sexuality is the impulse of life replicating itself. He observes that some people have arrived at great inventions, accomplishments, or business successes with the covert intention, unknown perhaps even to themselves, of wooing or pleasing a partner. This volume provides sufficient instruction so that you can experiment with these principles on your own.

The Magic Ladder to Success is one of the briefest but also the most complete digest of Hill's full range of ideas. It is a wonderful entry point for newcomers and a refresher for veterans. It also provides a sense of the broadness of Hill's overall vision. May this book ignite some of your highest efforts and ideas.

Introductory Statement

by the Author

For almost a quarter of a century I have been engaged in writing this book.

The task could not have been completed in less time for several reasons, not the least important of which is the fact that I had to inform myself, through years of research, as to what other men had discovered in connection with the causes of failure and success.

Another important reason why my labors have covered nearly a quarter of a century is the fact that I felt it necessary to prove that I could make the Law of Success philosophy work for myself before offering it to others.

I was born in the mountains of the South, in the midst of poverty and illiteracy. For three generations preceding me my ancestors, on both sides of the house, were contented to live in poverty and ignorance, and I would have followed in their footsteps had not my stepmother planted in my mind the seed of *desire* to whip poverty and illiteracy.

Nearly thirty years ago my stepmother made a remark which found a permanent lodging place in my mind, and to that remark may be traced the cause of my labors which have resulted in the completion of the Law of Success philosophy described in this book.

My stepmother was a woman of education, and came from a family with a long cultural record. Poverty and illiteracy irritated her, and she was not backward about saying so. She voluntarily assumed the task of planting ambition in our family, starting with my father, whom she sent away to college at the age of forty, while she managed what passed for a "farm" and a little country store that we owned, not to mention the support of five children, three of her own and my brother and myself.

Her example made a deep and lasting impression upon my mind!

From her I got my first impression of the value of a *definite major aim*, and later that impression became so obviously essential as one of the factors of success that I gave it second place in the list of seventeen principles outlined in this book.

When I began organizing the material for the Law of Success, I had no intention of creating a philosophy such as that described in this volume. My purpose, in the beginning, was to inform myself as to how other people had acquired wealth, so that I might follow their example.

But as the years passed I found myself becoming more eager for knowledge than for wealth, until my thirst for knowledge became so great that I practically lost sight of the original motive of financial gain which started me in search of knowledge.

In addition to the influence of my stepmother, I was fortunate enough to meet Dr. Alexander Graham Bell and Andrew Carnegie, who not only further influenced me to continue my research, but supplied me with much of the important scientific data which went into the building of the Law of Success philosophy.

Later I met Dr. Elmer Gates and many of the other men of recognized ability whom I have mentioned on another page, who not only encouraged me to continue my labor of building a philosophy of success, but gave me full benefit of their own rich experiences as their personal contribution to my task.

I have mentioned these details for what I believe to be a very important reason, namely, the fact that the difference between success and failure is often (if not, in fact, always) determined by definite environmental influences which may be usually traced to *one person*.

In my case this person was my stepmother.

Except for her influence in planting the seed of ambition in my mind, I never would have written a philosophy of success that is now rendering useful service to tens of thousands of people in every civilized country on earth.

Unfortunately, I shall never be able to ascertain the exact number of people who will receive from my work the inspiration that will lead to great achievement, but I do know, from what I have already seen in this direction, that the number will be stupendous. Perhaps it would be no exaggeration to say that no less than 10,000 people have already found, through this philosophy, the road to success.

While the Law of Success was still in the experimental stage, and as a part of my plan for giving it a practical trial before publishing it in textbooks, I personally passed it on, through lectures, to no less than 100,000 people. Many whom I know to have received their first impulse of ambition from these lectures have since become wealthy, although some of them may have lost sight of the cause of their prosperity, while others perhaps would not be generous enough to admit that my labor had marked important turning points in their lives.

My belief that this philosophy of success is destined to bring prosperity to almost countless thousands of people throughout the world is based upon what I have seen happen in the past, and upon very definite plans which I have formulated for teaching it.

I hope to have, very soon, able teachers in every city in America who will conduct schools of instruction for the purpose of teaching the Law of Success. I am engaged at this time in training teachers, and it is my aim to continue this work. For this purpose I have acquired a beautiful, six-hundred-acre estate in the Catskill Mountains, one hundred miles from New York City, where my school and headquarters will eventually be located. My teachers will be recruited from students of this philosophy who show, by their records, unusual aptitude for this sort of work.

The Law of Success will be translated into many foreign languages and taught in other countries. One of my most prominent students, who is a moving picture producer of more than ordinary ability, is planning the production of a series of talking pictures based upon the Law of Success textbooks. Through these pictures he will plant the seed of this philosophy in millions of minds.

Quite aside from my own program for the distribution of the Law of Success textbooks throughout the world, there is another, and, I believe, a more vital reason why this philosophy is destined to play an important part in the lives of great numbers of people. I have reference to the state of unrest which is manifesting itself, not only here in America, but throughout the world.

Since the World War, millions of people have been fired with ambition to whip poverty and to gain for themselves better stations in life. Moreover, this is most decidedly an age of scientific discovery, which has put sound legs under the seventeen principles of the Law of Success, thus giving it a standing that it did not enjoy fifteen years ago.

On account of the world unrest which is so prevalent to-day, there is a very definite demand for an "evangelism" of success that will inspire people with higher hopes and ambitions for personal achievement.

For the reasons here stated, I have arrived at last at an altitude on the mountain of life from which I may look backward into the valleys of struggle and hardship, poverty, and failure through which I have passed, with a feeling that I have not altogether lived in vain; that the punishment I have undergone has been more than offset by the joy and prosperity I have helped others to obtain.

Turning in the other direction, I can see that the summit of the mountain of success is still far in the distance and far from being finished and that my work is barely more than begun.

Not long ago I received a letter from a former president of the United States, who congratulated me upon sticking to my job for a quarter of a century, and suggested that I must feel very proud to have "arrived" at the top of the mountain of success in time to enjoy the fruits of my labors. His letter brought to my mind the thought that one never "arrives," if one continues to search for knowledge, because we no sooner reach the top of one peak than we discover that there are still higher mountains yet to be scaled in the distance.

No, I have not "arrived," but I have found happiness in abundance and financial prosperity sufficient for my needs, *solely through haring lost myself in service to others who were earnestly struggling to find themselves*. It seems worthy of mention that I did not prosper greatly until I became more concerned about spreading the Law of Success philosophy where it would help others than I was about accumulating money.

In this manner, with apologies for the personal references, would I acquaint you with the motive and the influence which started me on the work of organizing the philosophy described in this book.

Acknowledgment of Help Rendered in the Preparation of the Material That Has Gone into This Book

This volume is the result of an analysis of the life work of over one hundred men and women who have attained outstanding success in their respective callings and of over 20,000 men and women who were classed as failures.

In his labors of research and analysis the author received valuable assistance, either in person or by studying their life work, from the following men:

Henry Ford	Harvey S. Firestone
John Burroughs	John D. Rockefeller
Luther Burbank	Charles M. Schwab
Thomas A. Edison	Woodrow Wilson

Darwin P. Kingsley

Wm. Wrigley, Jr.

A.D. Lasker

E. A. Filene

James J. Hill

Dr. Glenn Frank

Capt. Geo. M. Alexander

Hugh Chalmers

John Wanamaker

Marshall Field

Edward W. Bok

Cyrus H. K. Curtis

George W. Perkins

Henry L. Doherty

George S. Parker

Gen. Rufus A. Ayers

Judge Elbert H. Gary

William Howard Taft

John W. Davis

Samuel Insull

Judge Daniel T. Wright

E. W. Woolworth

Elbert Hubbard

O. H. Harriman

Edwin C. Barnes

E. H. Harriman

Gov. Robt. L. Taylor

Wilbur Wright

George Eastman

William H. French

Charles P. Stienmetz

John H. Patterson

E. M. Statler

Don R. Mellett

Theodore Roosevelt

Dr. E. W. Strickler

Stuart Austin Wier

Harris F. Williams

Dr. Alexander Graham
  Bell

Of the men named, perhaps Henry Ford and Andrew Carnegie should be acknowledged as having contributed most to the building of this philosophy, for the reason that it was Mr. Carnegie who first suggested writing it and Henry Ford whose life work has supplied much of the material that has gone into its organization and served, in other ways, to prove the soundness of the entire philosophy.

Many of the men who supplied the author of the Law of Success with the most valuable portion of the data which have gone into the building of this philosophy have died before it was completed. To those who are still living, the author here makes grateful acknowledgment of the service they have rendered him, without which cooperation this philosophy never could have been completed.

—The Author.

How to Read This Book for Profit

Experience with many tens of thousands of people who have attended lectures by the author of the Law of Success and with the thousands of people who have read the eight textbooks in which this philosophy has been presented has brought to light the fact that the philosophy stimulates the mind and causes the birth of scores of ideas.

As you read this book you will observe, as thousands of others have done, that ideas will begin to "flash" into your mind. Capture these ideas, with the aid of a notebook and pencil, as they may lead you to the attainment of your coveted goal in life. Many students of this philosophy have created valuable inventions while reading the Law of Success textbooks. Clergymen have been inspired by this philosophy to write sermons which lifted them to great heights of eloquence. The Law of Success philosophy is a mind fertilizer. It will cause the mind to function as a magnet that will attract brilliant ideas.

The value of this book is not in its own pages, but it lies in your own reaction to that which you read on these pages. Any brain that can create new ideas in abundance is capable, also, of organizing great power! The main purpose of the Law of Success philosophy is to stimulate the *imaginative* faculties of the brain so they will readily create new and usable ideas for any emergency in life.

Read this book with pencil in hand, and as you read, underscore all statements which cause new ideas to "flash" into your mind. This method will serve to fix such ideas in your mind permanently. You cannot assimilate the entire subject matter of this philosophy at one reading of this book. Read it many times, and at each reading follow the habit of marking the lines which inspire new ideas.

This procedure will reveal to you one of the great mysteries of the human mind by introducing you to a source of knowledge which cannot be described adequately to any except those who have discovered this source for themselves. *In this statement lies a hint of the nature of the secret of success which the Law of Success philosophy has handed over to so many of its students throughout the world!* No one may ever come into possession of this secret except by the method of procedure here described.

The Seventeen Factors of Which the Law of Success Is Composed

⁓

This basic Reading Course presents the principles through which success may be attained. At the outset let us define success as:

"The *power* with which to acquire whatever one wants without violating the rights of others."

The factors through which power may be acquired and used in harmony with the above definition are seventeen in number, viz:

1. The Master Mind
2. A Definite Chief Aim
3. Self-Confidence
4. The Habit of Saving
5. Imagination
6. Initiative and Leadership

7. Enthusiasm
8. Self-Control
9. Doing More than Paid For
10. A Pleasing Personality
11. Accurate Thinking
12. Co-operation
13. Concentration
14. Profiting by Failures
15. Tolerance
16. The Golden Rule
17. The Habit of Health

The purpose of this Reading Course is to describe how one may apply these seventeen factors so as to acquire personal power for use in any calling and for the solution of all of one's economic problems. Let us begin this description by a complete analysis of each of these seventeen factors.

THE
MAGIC
LADDER
TO
SUCCESS

The Master Mind

The Master Mind principle may be defined as "A composite mind, consisting of two or more individual minds working in perfect harmony, with a definite aim in view."

Keep in mind the definition of success, which is attainable through the application of *power*, and you will more quickly grasp the meaning of the term "Master Mind," as it will be immediately obvious that a group of two or more minds, working in harmony, and perfectly coordinated, will create power in abundance.

All success is achieved through the application of *power*. The starting point, however, may be described as a *burning desire* for the achievement of some specific, definite objective.

Just as the oak tree, in the embryo, sleeps within the acorn, *success* begins in the form of an intense *desire*. Out of strong desires grow the motivating forces which cause men to cherish hopes, build plans, develop courage, and stimulate their minds to a highly intensified degree of *action* in pursuit of some *definite* plan or purpose.

Desire, then, is the starting point of all human achievement. There is nothing back of desire except the stimuli through which *strong desire* is fanned into a hot flame of *action.* These stimuli are known and have been included as a part of the Law of Success philosophy described in this book.

It has been said, and not without reason, that one may have anything one wants, within reasonable limitations, providing one *wants it badly enough!* Anyone who is capable of stimulating the mind to an intense state of *desire* is capable also of more than average achievement in the pursuit of that desire. It must be remembered that *wishing* for a thing is not the same as *desiring* it with such intensity that out of this desire grow impelling forces of action which drive one to build plans and put those plans to work. A wish is merely a passive form of desire. Most people never advance beyond the "wishing" stage.

The Basic Motivating Forces Which Underlie All Human Action

There are eight basic motivating forces, one or more of which is the starting point of all noteworthy human achievement. These motivating forces are:

1. The urge of self-preservation
2. The desire for sexual contact
3. The desire for financial gain
4. The desire for life after death
5. The desire for fame; to possess *power*
6. The urge of *love* (separate and distinct from sex urge)
7. The desire for revenge (prevalent in the more undeveloped minds)
8. The desire to indulge one's egotism

Men make use of great power only when urged by one or more of these eight basic motives. The imaginative forces of the human mind become active only when spurred on by the stimulation of well-defined *motive!* Master salesmen have discovered that all salesmanship is based upon an appeal to one or more of these eight basic motives which impel men and women to action. Without this discovery no one could become a master salesman.

What is salesmanship? It is the presentation of an idea, plan, or suggestion which gives the prospective purchaser a strong motive for making a purchase. The able salesman never asks a purchaser to buy without presenting a *well-defined motive* as to why the purchase should be made.

Knowledge of merchandise or service offered by the salesman, of itself, is not sufficient to make a master salesman. The offering must be accompanied by a thorough description of the motive which should prompt the purchaser to buy. The most effective sales plan is one which appeals to the prospective purchaser through the greatest number of the eight basic motives and crystallizes these motives into a *burning desire* for the object offered for sale.

The eight basic motives serve not only as the basis of appeal to other minds, where co-operative action from other people is sought, but they serve also as the starting point of *action* in one's own mind. Men of ordinary ability become supermen when aroused by some outward or inner stimulant which harnesses one or more of the eight basic motives for action.

Bring a man face to face with the possibility of death, in a sudden emergency, and he will develop physical strength and imaginative strategy of which he would not be capable under the influence of a less urgent motive for action.

When driven by the natural desire for sexual contact, men will build plans, use strategy, develop imagination, and indulge in action in a thousand different ways of which they are not capable without the urge of this desire.

The desire for financial gain often lifts men of mediocre ability into positions of great power because this desire causes them to build plans, develop imagination, and indulge in forms of action in which they would not engage without this motive of gain. The desire for fame and for personal power over others is easily discernible as the chief motivating force in the lives of leaders in every walk of life.

The animalistic desire for revenge often drives men to build the most intricate and ingenious plans for carrying out their objective.

Love for the opposite sex (and sometimes for the same sex) serves as a mind stimulant that drives men to almost unbelievable heights of achievement.

The desire for life after death is such a strong motivating force that it not only drives men to both constructive and destructive extremes in their search for a plan by which this perpetuation may be brought about, but it also develops highly effective leadership ability, evidence of which may be found in the life work of practically all the founders of religion.

If you would achieve great success, plant in your mind a strong motive!

Millions of people struggle all the days of their lives with no stronger motive than that of being able to acquire the necessities of life, such as food, shelter, and clothing. Now and then a man will step out of the ranks of this great army and *demand* of himself and of the world more than a mere living. He will motivate himself with the strong *desire* for fortune, and presto! as if by the hand of magic, his financial status changes and he begins to turn his action into cash.

Power and success are synonomous terms. Success is not attained through honesty alone, as some would have us believe. The poor-houses are filled with people who, perhaps, were honest enough. They failed to accumulate money because they lacked the knowledge of how to acquire and use *power!*

The Master Mind principle described in this lesson is the medium through which all personal power is applied. For this reason, every known mind stimulant, and every basic motive which inspires action in all human endeavor, has been mentioned in this chapter.

The Two Forms of Power

There are two forms of power which we shall analyze in this lesson. One is mental power, and it is acquired through the process of thought. It is expressed through definite plans of action, as the result of organized knowledge. The ability to think, plan, and act through well-organized procedure is the starting point of all mental power.

The other form of power is physical. It is expressed through natural laws, in the form of electrical energy, gravitation, steam pressure, etc. In this lesson we shall analyze both mental and physical power, and explain the relationship between the two.

Knowledge, alone, is not power. *Great personal power* is acquired only through the harmonious co-operation of a number of people who I concentrate their efforts upon some definite plan.

The Nature of Physical Power

The state of advancement known as "civilization" is but the measure of knowledge which the race has accumulated. Among the useful knowledge organized by man, he has discovered and cataloged the eighty-odd physical elements of which all material forms in the universe consist.

By study, and analysis, and accurate measurements man has discovered the "bigness" of the material side of the universe as represented by planets, suns, and stars, some of which are known to be over one million times as large as the little earth on which he lives.

On the other hand, man has discovered the "littleness" of the physical forms which constitute the universe by reducing the eighty-odd physical elements to molecules, atoms, and finally to the smallest particle, the electron. An electron cannot be seen; it is but a center of force consisting of a positive or a negative. The electron is the beginning of everything of a physical nature.

Molecules, Atoms, and Electrons

To understand the process through which knowledge is gathered, organized and classified, it seems essential for the student to begin with the smallest and simplest particles of physical matter, because these are the A B C's with which Nature has constructed the entire physical portion of the universe.

The molecule consists of atoms, which are said to be invisible particles of matter revolving continuously with the speed of lightning, on exactly the same principle that the earth revolves on its axis.

These little particles of matter known as atoms, which revolve in one continuous circuit, in the molecule, are said to be made up of electrons, the smallest particles of physical matter. As already stated, the electron is nothing but two forms of force. The electron is uniform, of but one class, size, and nature. Thus in a grain of sand or a drop of water is duplicated the entire principle upon which the whole universe operates.

How stupendous! You may gather some slight idea of the magnitude of it all the next time you eat a meal by remembering that every article of food you eat, the plate on which you eat it, the tableware and the table itself, are, in final analysis, but a collection of *electrons*.

In the world of physical matter, whether one is looking at the largest star that floats through the heavens or the smallest grain of sand to be found on earth, the object under observation is but an organized collection of molecules, atoms, and electrons revolving at inconceivable speed.

Every, particle of physical matter is in a continuous state of highly agitated motion. Nothing is ever still, although nearly all physical matter may appear, to the physical eye, to be motionless. There is no "solid" physical matter. The hardest piece of steel is but an organized mass of revolving molecules, atoms, and electrons. Moreover, the electrons in a piece of steel are of the same nature, and move at the same rate of speed, as the electrons in gold, silver, brass, or pewter.

The eighty-odd forms of physical matter appear to be different from one another, and they are different, because they are made up of different combinations of atoms (although the electrons in those atoms are always the same, except that some electrons are positive and some are negative, meaning that some carry a positive charge of electrification while others carry a negative charge).

Through the science of chemistry, matter may be broken up into atoms which are, within themselves, unchangeable. The eighty-odd elements are created through, and by reason of, combining and changing the positions of the atoms. To illustrate the modus operandi of chemistry through which this change of atomic position is wrought, in terms of modern science:

"Add four electrons (two positive and two negative) to the hydrogen atom, and you have the element lithium; knock out of the lithium atom (composed of three positive and three negative electrons) one positive and one negative electron, and you have one atom of helium (composed of two positive and two negative electrons)."

Thus it may be seen that the eighty-odd physical elements of the universe differ from one another only in the number of electrons composing their atoms, and the number and arrangement of those atoms in the molecules of each element.

As an illustration, an atom of mercury contains eighty positive charges (electrons) on its nucleus, and eighty negative outlying charges (electrons). If the chemist were to expel two of its positive electrons, it would instantly become the metal known as platinum. If the chemist then could go a step further and take from it a negative ("planetary") electron, the mercury atom would then have lost two positive electrons and one negative; that is, one positive charge on the whole; hence it would retain seventy-nine positive charges on the nucleus and seventy-nine outlying negative electrons, thereby becoming *gold!*

The formula through which this electronic change might be produced has been the object of diligent search by the alchemists all back down the ages, and of the modern chemists of to-day.

It is a fact known to every chemist that literally tens of thousands of synthetic substances may be composed out of only four kinds of atoms, viz., hydrogen, oxygen, nitrogen, and carbon.

The electron is the universal particle with which Nature builds all material forms, from a grain of sand to the largest star that floats through space. The electron is Nature's "building block" out of which she erects an oak tree or a pine, a rock of sandstone or granite, a mouse or an elephant.

Some of the ablest thinkers have reasoned that the earth on which we live, and every material particle of the earth, began with two atoms which attached themselves to each other, and through hundreds of millions of years of flight through space, kept contracting and accumulating other atoms until, step by step, the earth was formed. This, they point out, would account for the various and differing stratums of the earth's substances, such as the coal beds, the iron ore deposits, the gold and silver deposits, the copper deposits, etc.

They reason that, as the earth whirled through space, it contracted groups of various kinds of nebulae, which it promptly appropriated through the law of magnetic attraction. There is much to be seen, in the earth's surface composition, to support this theory, although there may be no positive evidence of its soundness.

These facts concerning the smallest analyzable particles of matter have been briefly referred to as a starting point from which we shall undertake to ascertain how to develop and apply the laws of *power*.

It has been noticed that all matter is in a constant state of vibration or motion; that the molecule is made up of rapidly moving particles called atoms, which, in turn, are made up of rapidly moving particles called electrons.

The Vibrating Principle of Matter

In every particle of matter there is an invisible force which causes the atoms to move around one another at an inconceivable rate of speed.

This is a form of energy which has never been analyzed. Thus far it has baffled the entire scientific world. By many scientists it is believed to be the same energy as that which we call electricity. Others prefer to call it vibration. It is believed by some investigators that the rate of speed with which this force (call it whatever you will) moves determines the nature of the physical objects of the universe.

One rate of vibration causes what is known as sound. The human ear can detect only the sound which is produced through from thirty-two to thirty-eight thousand vibrations per second.

As the rate of vibrations per second increases above that which we call sound, they begin to manifest themselves in the form of heat. Heat begins with about one million and a half vibrations per second.

Still higher up the scale, vibrations begin to register in the form of light. Three million vibrations per second create violet light. Above this number vibration sheds ultra-violet rays (which are invisible to the naked eye) and other invisible radiations.

And still higher up the scale, just how high no one at present seems to know, vibrations create the power with which man *thinks*.

It is the belief of this author that the portion of vibration out of which grows all known forms of energy is universal in nature; that the "fluid" portion of sound is the same as the "fluid" portion of light, the difference in effect between sound and light being only a difference in rate of vibration; also that the "fluid" portion of thought is exactly the same as that in sound, heat, and light, excepting the number of vibrations per second.

Just as there is but one form of physical matter of which the earth and all the other planets, suns, and stars are composed—the electron—so is there but one form of "fluid" energy which causes all matter to remain in a constant state of rapid motion.

Air and Ether

The vast space between the suns, moons, stars, and other planets of the universe is filled with a form of energy known as ether. It is this author's belief that the "fluid" energy, which keeps all the particles of matter in motion, is the same as the universal "fluid" known as ether, which fills all the space of the universe. Within a certain distance of the earth's surface, estimated by some to be about fifty miles, there exists what is called air, which is a gaseous substance composed of oxygen and nitrogen. Air is a conductor of sound vibrations, but a nonconductor of light and the higher vibrations, which are carried by the ether. The ether is a conductor of all vibrations from sound to thought.

Air is a localized substance which performs, in the main, the service of feeding all animal and plant life with oxygen and nitrogen, without which neither could exist. Nitrogen is one of the chief necessities of plant life, and oxygen one of the mainstays of animal life. Near the top of very high mountains the air becomes very light, because it contains but little nitrogen, which is the reason why plant life cannot exist there. On the other hand, the "light" air found in the high altitude consists largely of oxygen which is the chief reason why tubercular patients are sent to high altitudes.

Even this brief statement concerning molecules, atoms, electrons, air, ether, and the like may be heavy reading, but, as will be seen shortly, this introduction plays an essential part as the foundation of this philosophy of success.

Do not become discouraged if the description of this foundation appears to have none of the thrilling effects of a modern tale of fiction. You are seriously engaged in finding out what are your available powers and how to organize and apply these powers. To successfully complete this discovery you must combine determination, persistency, and a well-defined *desire* to gather and organize knowledge.

The Nature of Mental Power

The late Dr. Alexander Graham Bell, inventor of the long distance telephone and one of the accepted authorities on the subject of vibration, is here introduced in support of the statements in this volume concerning the subject of vibration, which is the basis of all mental power, and of all thought.

"Suppose you have the power to make an iron rod vibrate with any desired frequency in a dark room. At first, when vibrating slowly, its movement will be indicated by only one sense, that of touch. As soon as the vibrations increase, a low sound will emanate from it and it will appeal to two senses.

"At about thirty-two thousand vibrations to the second the sound will be loud and shrill; but at forty thousand vibrations it will be silent and the movements of the rod will not be perceived by touch. Its movements will be perceived by no ordinary human sense.

"From this point up to about one million and a half vibrations per second, we have no sense that can appreciate any effect of the intervening vibrations. After that stage is reached, movement is indicated first by the sense of temperature and then, when the rod becomes red hot, by the sense of sight. At three million vibrations it sheds violet fight. Above that it sheds ultra-violet rays and other invisible radiations, some of which can be perceived by instruments and employed by us.

"Now it has occurred to me that there must be a great deal to be learned about the effect of those vibrations in the great gap where ordinary human senses are unable to hear, see or feel the movement. The power to send wireless messages by ether vibrations lies in that gap, but the gap is so great that it seems there must be much more. You must make machines practically to supply new senses, as the wireless instruments do.

"Can it be said, when you think of that great gap, that there are not many forms of vibrations that may give us results as wonderful as, or even more wonderful than, the wireless waves? It seems to me that in this gap lie the vibrations which we have assumed to be given off by our brain and nerve cells when we think. But then, again, they may be higher up in the scale beyond the vibrations that produce the ultraviolet rays. (Author's note: The last sentence suggests the theory held by this author.)

"Do we need a wire to carry these vibrations? Will they not pass through the ether without a wire, just as the wireless waves do? How will they be perceived by the recipient? Will he hear a series of signals, or will he find that another man's thoughts have entered into his brain?

"We may indulge in some speculations based on what we know of the wireless waves, which, as I have said, are all we can recognize of a vast series of vibrations which theoretically must exist. If the thought waves are similar to the wireless waves, they must pass from the brain and flow endlessly around the world and the universe. The body and the skull and other solid obstacles would form no obstruction to their passage, as they pass through the ether which surrounds the molecules of every substance, no matter how solid and dense.

"You ask if there would not be constant interference and confusion if other people's thought were flowing through our brains and setting up thoughts in them that did not originate with ourselves?

"How do you know that other men's thoughts are not interfering with yours now? I have noticed a good many phenomena of mind disturbances that I have never been able to explain. For instance, there is the inspiration or the discouragement that a speaker feels in addressing an audience. I have experienced this many times in my life and have never been able to define exactly the physical causes of it.

"Many recent scientific discoveries, in my opinion, point to a day, not far distant perhaps, when men will read one another's thoughts, when thoughts will be conveyed directly from brain to brain without the intervention of speech, writing or any of the present known methods of communication.

"It is not unreasonable to look forward to a time when we shall see without eyes, hear without ears, and talk without tongues.

"Briefly, the hypothesis that mind can communicate directly with mind rests on the theory that thought or vital force is a form of electrical disturbance, that it can be taken up by induction and transmitted to a distance either through a wire or simply through the all pervading ether, as in the case of wireless telegraph waves.

"There are many analogies which suggest that thought is of the nature of an electrical disturbance. A nerve which is of the same substance as the brain is an excellent conductor of the electric current. When we first passed an electrical current through the nerves of a dead man, we were shocked and amazed to see him sit up and move. The electrified nerves produced contraction of the muscles very much as in life.

"The nerves appear to act upon the muscles very much as the electric current acts upon an electromagnet. The current magnetizes a bar of iron placed at right angles to it, and the nerves produce, through the intangible current of vital force that flows through them, contraction of the muscular fibers that are arranged at right angles to them.

"It would be possible to cite many reasons why thought and vital force may be regarded as of the same nature as electricity. The electric I current is held to be a wave motion of the ether—the hypothetical substance that fills all space and pervades all substances. We believe that there must be ether, because without it the electric current could not pass through a vacuum, or sunlight through space. It is reasonable I to believe that only a wave motion of a similar character can produce the phenomena of thought and vital force. We may assume that the brain cells act as a battery and that the current produced flows along the nerves.

"But does it end there? Does it hot pass out of the body in waves which flow around the world unperceived by our senses, just as the wireless waves passed unperceived before Hertz and others discovered their existence?"

Every Mind Both a Broadcasting and a Receiving Station

This author has proved, to his own satisfaction at least, that every human brain is both a broadcasting and a receiving station for vibrations of thought frequency.

If this theory should turn out to be a fact, and methods of reasonable control should be established, imagine the part it would play in the gathering, classifying, and organizing of knowledge. The possibility, much less the probability of such a reality, staggers the mind of man!

Thomas Paine was one of the great minds of the American Revolutionary period. To him more, perhaps, than to any other one person, we owe both the beginning and the happy ending of the Revolution, for it was his keen mind that both helped in drawing up the Declaration of Independence and in persuading the signers of that document to translate it into terms of reality.

In speaking of the source of his great storehouse of knowledge, Paine thus described it:

"Any person who has made observations on the state of progress of the human mind, by observing his own, cannot but have observed that there are two distinct classes of what are called thoughts: Those that we produce in ourselves by reflection and the act of thinking, and those that bolt into the mind of their own accord. I have always made it a rule to treat these voluntary visitors with civility, taking care to examine, as well as I was able, if they were worth entertaining; and it is from them I have acquired almost all the knowledge that I have. As to the learning that any person gains from school education, it serves (only like a small capital, to put him in the way of beginning learning for himself afterwards. Every person of learning is finally his own teacher, the reason for which is, that principles, being of a distinct quality to circumstances, cannot be impressed upon the memory; their place of mental residence is the understanding, and they are never so lasting as when they begin by conception."

> Putting ideas to work is a profitable business, but it makes a slight difference whether the ideas were created by you or by someone else.

In the foregoing words Paine, the great American patriot and philosopher, described a phenomenon which at one time or another is the experience of every person. Who is so unfortunate as not to have received positive evidence that thoughts and even complete ideas will "pop" into the mind from the outside sources?

What means of conveyance is there for such visitors except the ether? Ether fills the boundless space of the universe. It is the medium of conveyance for all known forms of vibration such as sound, light, and heat. Why would it not be, also, the medium of conveyance of the vibration of thought?

Every mind, or brain, is directly connected with every other brain by means of the ether. Every thought released by any brain may be instantly picked up and interpreted by all other brains that are en rapport with the sending brain. This author is as sure of this fact as he is that the chemical formula H_2O will produce water.

Nor is the probability of ether being a conveyer of thought from mind to mind the most astounding of its performances. It is the belief of this author that every thought vibration released by any brain is picked up by the ether and kept in motion in circuitous wave lengths corresponding in length to the intensity of the energy used in its release; that these vibrations remain in motion forever; that they are one of the two sources from which thoughts which "pop" into one's mind emanate, the other source being direct and immediate contact through the ether with the brain releasing the thought vibration.

Thus it will be seen that if this theory is a fact, the boundless space of the whole universe is now and will continue to become literally a library wherein may be found all the thoughts released by mankind.

The author is here laying the foundation for one of the most important hypotheses enumerated in this chapter.

According to men of science, most of the useful knowledge to which the human race has become heir has been preserved and accurately recorded in Nature's Bible.

By turning back the pages of this unalterable Bible, man has read the story of the terrific struggle through and out of which the present civilization has grown. The pages of this Bible are made up of the physical elements of which this earth and the other planets consist, and of the ether which fills all space.

By turning back the pages written on stone and covered near the surface of this earth on which he lives, man has uncovered the bones, skeletons, footprints, and other unmistakable evidence of the history of animal life on this earth, planted there for his enlightenment and guidance by the hand of Mother Nature throughout unbelievable periods of time. The evidence is plain and unmistakable. The great stone pages of Nature's Bible found on this earth, and the endless pages of that Bible represented by the ether wherein all past human thought has been recorded, constitute an authentic source of communication between the Creator and man. This Bible was begun before man had reached the thinking stage; indeed, before man had reached the amoeba (one-cell animal) stage of development.

This Bible is above and beyond the power of man to alter. Moreover, it tells its story in universal language which all who have eyes may read. Nature's Bible, from whence we have derived all the knowledge that is worth knowing, is one that no man may alter or in any manner tamper with.

The most marvelous discovery yet made by man is the recently discovered radio principle, which operates through the aid of ether; an important portion of Nature's Bible. Imagine the ether picking up the ordinary vibration of sound, and transforming (stepping up the rate of vibration) that vibration from audio-frequency into radio-frequency, carrying it to a properly attuned receiving station and there transforming it back into its original form of audio-frequency, all in the flash of a second. It should surprise no one that such a force could gather up the vibration of thought and keep that vibration in motion forever.

The established and known fact of instantaneous transmission of sound, through the agency of the ether, by means of the modern radio apparatus, removes the theory of transmission of thought vibrations from mind to mind from the possible to the probable.

The Master Mind

We come now to the next step in the description of the ways and means by which one may gather, classify, and organize useful knowledge, through harmonious alliance of two or more minds, out of which grows a Master Mind.

The term "Master Mind" is abstract, and has no counterpart in the field of known facts, except to a small number of people who have made a careful study of the effect of one mind upon other minds.

This author has searched in vain through all the textbooks and essays available on the subject of the human mind, but nowhere has been found even the slightest reference to the principle here described as the "Master Mind." The term first came to the attention of the author through an interview with Andrew Carnegie, in the manner described in another chapter.

Chemistry of the Mind

It is this author's belief that the mind is made up of the same energy as that which constitutes the ether which fills the universe. It is a fact, as well known to the layman as to the man of scientific investigation, that some minds clash the moment they come in contact with each other. Between the two extremes of natural antagonism and natural affinity growing out of the meeting or contacting of minds, there is a wide range of possibility for varying reactions of mind upon mind.

Some minds are so naturally adapted to each other that "love at first sight" is the inevitable outcome of the contact. Who has not known of such an experience? In other cases minds are so antagonistic that violent mutual dislike shows itself at first meeting. These results occur without a word being spoken, and without the slightest signs of any of the usual causes for love and hate acting as a stimulus.

It is quite probable that the "mind" is made up of a substance or energy, call it what you will, similar to (if not, in fact, the same substance) the ether. When two minds come close enough to each other to form a contact, the mixing of the units of this "mind stuff" (let us call it the electrons of the ether) sets up a chemical reaction and starts vibrations which affect the two individuals pleasantly or unpleasantly.

The effect of the meeting of two minds is obvious to even the most casual observer. Every effect must have a cause! What could be more reasonable than to suspect that the cause of the change in mental attitude between the two minds, which have just come in contact, is none other than the disturbance of the electrons or units of each mind in the process of rearranging themselves in the new field created by the contact?

For the purpose of establishing this philosophy upon a sound foundation, we have gone a long way toward success by admitting that the meeting or coming in close contact of two minds sets up in each of those minds a certain noticeable "effect" or state of mind quite different from the one existing immediately prior to the contact. While it is desirable, it is not essential to know what is the "cause" of this reaction of mind upon mind. That the reaction takes place in every instance is a known fact, which gives us a starting point from which we pay show what is meant by the term "Master Mind."

A Master Mind may be created through the bringing together or blending, in a spirit of perfect harmony, of two or more minds. Out of this harmonious blending, the chemistry of the mind creates a third mind which may be appropriated and used by one or all of the individual minds. This Master Mind will remain available as long as the friendly, harmonious alliance between the individual minds exists. It will disintegrate and all evidence of its existence disappear the moment the friendly alliance is broken.

This principle of mind chemistry is the basis and cause of practically all the so-called "soul mate" and "eternal triangle" cases, so many of which unfortunately find their way into the divorce courts and meet with popular ridicule from ignorant and uneducated people who manufacture vulgarity and scandal out of one of the greatest of Nature's laws.

The entire civilized world knows that the first two or three years of association after marriage are often marked by much disagreement of a more or less petty nature. These are the years of "adjustment." If the marriage survives them, it is more than apt to become a permanent alliance. These facts no experienced married person will deny. Again we see the "effect" without understanding the "cause."

While there are other contributing causes, yet, in the main, lack of harmony during these early years of marriage is due to the slowness of the chemistry of the minds in blending harmoniously. Stated differently, the electrons or units of the energy called the mind are often neither extremely friendly nor antagonistic upon first contact; but through constant association they gradually adapt themselves in harmony, except in rare cases where association has the opposite effect of leading eventually to open hostility between these units.

It is a well-known fact that after a man and a woman have lived together for ten to fifteen years, they become practically indispensable to each other, even though there may not be the slightest evidence of the state of mind called love. Moreover, this association and relationship sexually not only develops a natural affinity between the two minds, but it actually causes the two people to take on a similar facial expression and to closely resemble each other in many other marked ways. Any competent analyst of human nature can easily go into a crowd of strange people and pick out the wife after having been introduced to her husband. The expression of the eyes, the contour of the faces, and the tone of the voices of the people who have long been associated in marriage become similar to a marked degree.

So marked is the effect of the chemistry of the human mind that any experienced public speaker may quickly interpret the manner in which his statements are accepted by his audience. Antagonism in the mind of but one person in an audience of one thousand may be readily detected by the speaker who has learned how to "feel" and register the effects of antagonism. Moreover, the public speaker can make these interpretations without observing or in any manner being influenced by the expression on the faces of those in his audience. On account of this fact, an audience may cause a speaker to rise to great heights of oratory, or heckle him into failure, without making a sound or denoting a single expression of satisfaction or dissatisfaction through the features of the face.

All "Master Salesmen" know the moment the "psychological time for closing" has arrived; not by what the prospective buyer says, but from the effect of the chemistry of his mind as interpreted or "felt" by the salesman. Words often belie the intentions of those speaking them, but a correct interpretation of the chemistry of the mind leaves no loophole for such a possibility. Every able salesman knows that the majority of buyers have a habit of affecting a negative attitude almost to the very climax of a sale.

Every able lawyer has developed a sixth sense with which he is enabled to "feel" his way through the most artfully selected words of the clever witness who is lying, and correctly interpret that which is in the mind of the witness through the chemistry of the mind. Many lawyers have developed this ability without knowing the real source of it; they possess the technique without the scientific understanding upon which it is based. Many salesmen have done the same thing.

One who is gifted in the art of correctly interpreting the chemistry of the minds of others may, figuratively speaking, walk in at the front door of the mansion of a given mind and leisurely explore the entire building, denoting all its details, walking out again with a complete picture of the interior of the building without the owner of the building so much as knowing that he has entertained a visitor. It will be observed, in the chapter on Accurate Thinking, that this principle may be put to a very practical use (having reference to the principle of the chemistry of the mind).

Enough has already been stated to introduce the principle of mind chemistry, and to prove, with the aid of the reader's own everyday experiences and casual observations that the moment two *minds* come within close range of each other, a noticeable mental change takes place in both, sometimes registering in the nature of antagonism and at other times registering in the nature of friendliness. Every mind has what might be termed an electric field. The nature of this field varies, depending upon the "mood" of the individual mind back of it, and upon the nature of the chemistry of the mind creating the "field."

It is believed by this author that the normal or natural condition of the chemistry of any individual mind is the result of his physical heredity, plus the nature of thoughts which have dominated that mind; that every mind is continuously changing to the extent that the individual's philosophy and general habits of thought change the chemistry of his or her mind. These principles the author *believes* to be true. That any individual may voluntarily change the chemistry of his or her mind so that it will either attract or repel all with whom it comes in contact is a *known fact!* Stated in another manner, any person may assume a mental attitude which will attract and please others or repel and antagonize them, and this without the aid of words, or facial expression, or other form of bodily movement or demeanor.

Go back, now, to the definition of a "Master Mind"—a *mind* which grows out of the blending and co-ordination of two or more minds, *in a spirit of perfect harmony,* and you will catch the full significance of the word "harmony" as it is here used. Two minds will not blend nor can they be co-ordinated unless the element of perfect harmony is present, wherein lies the secret of success or failure of practically all business and social partnerships.

Every sales manager and every military commander and every leader in any other walk of life understands the necessity of an "esprit de corps"—a spirit of common understanding and co-operation—in the attainment of success. This mass spirit of harmony of purpose is obtained through discipline, voluntary or forced, of such a nature that the individual minds become blended into a

"Master Mind," by which is meant that the chemistry of the individual minds is modified in such a manner that these minds blend and function as one.

The methods through which this "blending" process takes place are as numerous as are the individuals engaged in the various forms of leadership. Every leader has his or her own method of co-ordinating the minds of the followers. One will use force. Another uses persuasion. One will play upon the fear of penalties, while another plays upon rewards, in order to reduce the individual minds of given groups of people to where they may be blended into a mass mind. The student will not have to search deeply into history of statesmanship, politics, business, or finance, to discover the technique employed by the leaders in these fields in the process of blending the minds of individuals into a mass mind.

The really great leaders of the world, however, have been provided by nature with a combination of mind chemistry favorable as a nucleus of attraction for other minds. Napoleon was a notable example of a man possessing the magnetic type of mind which had a very decided tendency to attract all minds with which it came in contact. Soldiers followed Napoleon to certain death without flinching, because of the impelling or attracting nature of his personality, and that personality was nothing more nor less than the chemistry of his mind.

No group of minds can be blended into a "Master Mind" if one of the individuals of that group possesses an extremely negative, repellent mind. The negative and positive minds will not blend in the sense here described as a "Master Mind." Lack of knowledge of this fact has brought many an otherwise able leader to defeat.

Any leader who understands this principle of mind chemistry may temporarily blend the minds of practically any group of people, so that it will represent a mass mind, but the composition will disintegrate almost the very moment the leader's presence is removed from the group. The most successful life insurance sales organizations and other sales forces meet once a week, or more often, *for the purpose of merging the individual minds into a Master Mind which will, for a limited number of days, serve as a stimulus to the individual minds!*

It may be, and generally is, true that the leaders of these groups do not understand what actually takes place in these meetings, which are usually given over to talks by the leader and other members of the group; meanwhile the minds of the individuals are "contacting" and recharging one another.

The brain of a human being may be compared to an electric battery in that it will become exhausted or run down, causing the owner of it to feel despondent, discouraged and lacking in "pep." Who is so fortunate as never to have had such a feeling? The human brain, when in this depleted condition, must be recharged, and the manner in which this is done is through contact with a more vital mind or minds. The great leaders understand the necessity of this "recharging" process, and moreover, they understand how to accomplish this result. *This knowledge is the main feature which distinguishes a leader from a follower!*

Fortunate is the person who understands this principle sufficiently well to keep his or her brain vitalized or "recharged" by periodically contacting it with a more vital mind. Sexual contact is one of the most effective of the stimuli through which a mind may be recharged, providing the contact is intelligently made between man and woman who have genuine affection for each other. Any other sort of sexual relationship is a devitalizer of the mind.

Before passing away from the brief reference made to sexual contact as a means of revitalizing a depleted mind, it seems appropriate to call attention to the fact that all of the great leaders, in whatever walks of life they have arisen, have been and are people of highly sexed natures. (The word "sex" is a decent word. You'll find it in all the dictionaries.)

There is a growing tendency upon the part of the best informed physicians and other health practitioners to accept the theory that all diseases begin when the brain of the individual is in a depleted or devitalized state.

Stated in another way, it is a known fact that a person who has a perfectly vitalized brain is practically, if not entirely, immune from all manner of disease.

Every intelligent health practitioner, of whatever school or type, knows that "Nature," or the mind, cures disease in every instance where a cure is affected. Medicines, faith, laying on of hands, chiropractic, osteopathy, and all other forms of outside stimulant are nothing more than artificial aids to Nature, or, to state it correctly, mere methods of setting the chemistry of the mind into motion to the end that it readjusts the cells and tissues of the body, revitalizes the brain, and otherwise causes the human machine to function normally.

The most orthodox practitioner should admit the truth of this statement.

What, then, may be the possibilities of the future in the field of mind chemistry?

Through the principle of harmonious blending of minds, perfect health may be enjoyed. Through the aid of this same principle, sufficient power may be developed to solve the problems of economic necessity which constantly press upon every individual.

We may judge the future possibilities of mind chemistry by taking inventory of its past achievements, keeping in mind the fact that these achievements have been largely the result of accidental discovery and of chance groupings of minds. We are approaching the time when the professorate of the universities will teach mind chemistry the same as other subjects are now taught. Meanwhile, study and experimentation in connection with this subject open vistas of possibility for the individual student.

Mind Chemistry and Economic Power

That mind chemistry may be appropriately applied to the work-a-day affairs of the economic and commercial world is a demonstrable fact.

Through the blending of two or more minds, in a spirit of *perfect harmony*, the principle of mind chemistry may be made to develop sufficient power to enable the individuals whose minds have been thus blended to perform seemingly superhuman feats. Power is the force with which men achieve success in any undertaking. Power, in unlimited quantities, may be enjoyed by any group of men, or men and women, who possess the wisdom with which to submerge their own personalities and their own immediate individual interests, through the blending of their minds in a spirit of perfect harmony.

Observe the frequency with which the word "harmony" appears throughout this introduction! There can be no development of a "Master Mind" where this element of *perfect harmony* does not exist. The individual units of one mind will not blend with the individual units of another mind *until the two minds have been aroused and warmed, as it were, with a spirit of perfect harmony of purpose.* The moment two minds begin to take divergent roads of interest, the individual units of each mind separate, and the third element,

Is it not strange that nowhere in history do we find a record of one great man who attained his greatness through deceit, trickery, and by double-crossing his business, associates?

known as a "Master Mind" which grew out of the friendly or harmonious alliance, will disintegrate.

We come, now, to the study of some well-known men who have accumulated great power (also great fortunes) through the application of the Master Mind.

Let us begin with three great men who are known to be men of great achievement in their respective fields of business and professional endeavor.

Their names are Henry Ford, Thomas A. Edison, and Harvey Firestone.

Of the three Henry Ford is by far the most *powerful*, having reference to economic and financial power. Mr. Ford is the most powerful man now living on earth. Many who have studied Mr. Ford believe him to be the most powerful man who ever lived. As far as is known Mr. Ford is the only man now living, or who ever lived, with sufficient power to outwit the money trust of the

United States. Mr. Ford gathers millions of dollars with as great ease as a child fills its bucket with sand when playing on the beach. It has been said by those who were in position to know that Mr. Ford, if he needed it, could send out the call for money and gather in a billion dollars (a thousand million dollars) and have it available for use within one week. No one who knows of Ford's achievements doubts this. Those who know him well know that he could do it with no more effort than the average man expends in raising the money with which to pay a month's house rent.

Mr. Edison, as everyone knows, is a philosopher, scientist, and inventor. He is, perhaps, the keenest Bible student on earth; a student of Nature's Bible, however. Mr. Edison has such a keen insight into Mother Nature's Bible that he has harnessed and combined for the good of mankind, more of Nature's Laws than any person now living or who ever lived. It was he who brought together the point of a needle and a piece of revolving wax in such a way that the vibration of the human voice may be recorded and reproduced through the modem talking machine.

And it may be Edison or a man of his type, who will eventually enable man to pick up and correctly interpret the vibrations of thought which are now recorded in the boundless universe of ether, just as he has enabled man to record and reproduce the spoken word.

It was Edison who first harnessed the lightning and made it serve as a light for man's use, through the aid of the incandescent electric light bulb.

It was Edison who gave the world the modern moving picture.

These are but a few of his outstanding achievements. These modern "miracles," which he has performed in the very midst of the bright light of science, transcend all of the "miracles" described by Jules Verne and others in books of fiction.

Mr. Firestone is the moving spirit in the great Firestone Tire industry in Akron, Ohio. His industrial achievements are so well known wherever automobiles are used that no special comment on them seems necessary.

All three men began their careers, business and professional, without capital and with but little schooling of that type usually referred to as "education."

All three men are now well educated. All three are wealthy. All three are powerful. Now let us inquire into the source of their wealth and power. Thus far we have been dealing only with effect; the true philosopher wishes to understand the "cause" of a given effect.

It is a matter of general knowledge that Mr. Ford, Mr. Edison, and Mr. Firestone are close personal friends, and have been so for many years; that in former years they were in the habit of going away to the woods once a year for a period of rest, meditation, and recuperation.

But it is not generally known—it is a grave doubt if these three men, themselves, know it—that there exists between the three men a bond of harmony which has caused their minds to become blended into a "Master Mind" which is the real source of the power of each. This mass mind, growing out of the coordination of the individual minds of Ford, Edison, and Firestone, has enabled these men to "tune in" on forces and sources of knowledge with which most men are to no extent familiar.

If the student doubts either the principle or the effects here described, let him remember that more than half the theory here set forth is a known fact. For example, it is known that these three men have great power. It is known that they are wealthy. It is known that they began without capital and with but little schooling. It is known that they form periodic mind contacts. It is known that they are harmonious and friendly. It is known that their achievements are so outstanding as to make it impossible to compare these achievements with those of other men in their respective fields of activity.

All these "effects" are known to practically every schoolboy in the civilized world, therefore there can be no dispute as far as effects are concerned.

Of one fact connected with the "cause" of the achievements of Edison, Ford, and Firestone we may be sure, namely, that these achievements are in no way based upon trickery, deceit, or any other form of unnatural law. These men do not possess a stock of legerdemain. They work with natural laws which, for the most part, are well known to all economists and leaders in the field of science, with the possible exception of the law upon which chemistry of the mind is based. As yet chemistry of the mind is not sufficiently developed to be classed, by scientific men, in their catalogue of known laws.

A "Master Mind" may be created by any group of people who will co-ordinate their minds in a spirit of perfect harmony. The group may consist of any number from two upward. Best results appear available from the blending of six or seven minds.

It has been suggested that Jesus Christ discovered how to make use of the principle of mind chemistry, and that His seemingly miraculous performances grew out of the power He developed through the blending of the minds of His twelve disciples. It has been pointed out that when one of the disciples broke faith (Judas Iscariot) the "Master Mind" immediately disintegrated and Jesus met with the supreme catastrophe of His life.

When two or more people harmonize their minds and produce the effect known as a "Master Mind," each person in the group becomes vested with the power to contact with and gather knowledge through the "subconscious" minds of all the other members of the group. This power becomes immediately noticeable, having the effect of stimulating the mind to a higher rate of vibration, and otherwise evidencing itself in the form of a more vivid imagination and the consciousness of what appears to be a sixth sense. It is through this sixth sense that new ideas will "flash" into the mind. These ideas take on the nature and form of the subject dominating the mind of the individual. If the entire group has met for the purpose of discussing a given subject, ideas concerning that subject will come pouring into the minds of all present, as if an outside influence were dictating them. The minds of those participating in the "Master Mind" become as magnets, attracting ideas and thought stimuli of the most highly organized and practical nature, from—no one knows where!

The process of mind blending here described as a "Master Mind" may be likened to the act of one who connects many electric batteries to a single transmission wire, thereby "stepping up" the power passing over that fine by the amount of energy the batteries carry. Just so in the case of blending individual minds into a "Master Mind." Each mind, through the principle of mind chemistry, stimulates all the other minds in the group, until the mind energy thus becomes so great that it penetrates and connects with the universal energy known as ether, which, in turn, touches every atom of matter in the universe.

Every public speaker has felt the influence of mind chemistry, for it is a well-known fact that as soon as the individual minds of an audience become en rapport (attuned to the rate of vibration of the mind of the speaker) with the speaker, there is a noticeable increase of enthusiasm in the speaker's mind, and he often rises to heights of oratory which surprise all, including himself.

The first five to ten minutes of the average speech are devoted to what is known as "warming up." By this is meant the process through which the minds of the speaker and his audience are becoming blended in a spirit of *perfect harmony*.

Every speaker knows what happens when this state of "perfect harmony" fails to materialize upon the part of his audience.

The seemingly supernatural phenomena occurring in spiritualistic meetings are the result of the reaction, upon one another, of the minds in the group. These phenomena seldom begin to manifest themselves under ten to twenty minutes after the group is formed, for the reason that this is about the time required for the minds in the group to become harmonized or blended.

The "messages" received by members of a spiritualistic group probably come from one of two sources, or from both, namely:

First: From the vast storehouse of the subconscious mind of some member of the group, or,

Second: From the universal storehouse of the ether, in which, it is more than probable, all thought vibration is preserved.

Neither any known natural law nor human reason support the theory of communication with individuals who have died.

It is a known fact that any individual may explore the store of knowledge in another's mind, through this principle of mind chemistry, and it seems reasonable to suppose that this power may be extended to include contact with whatever vibrations are available in the ether, if there are any.

The theory that all the higher and more refined vibrations, such as thought, are preserved in the ether, grows out of the known fact that neither matter nor energy (the two known elements of the universe) may be either created or destroyed. It is reasonable to suppose that all vibrations, which have been "stepped up" sufficiently to be picked up and absorbed in the ether, will go on forever. The lower vibrations, which do not blend with or otherwise contact the ether, probably exist a natural life and die out.

All the so-called geniuses probably gained their reputations because, by mere chance or otherwise, they formed alliances with other minds which enabled them to "step up" their own mind vibrations to where they were enabled to contact the vast Temple of Knowledge recorded and filed in the ether of the universe. All of the great geniuses, as far as this author has been enabled to gather the facts, were highly sexed people. The fact that sexual contact is the greatest known mind stimulant lends color to the theory herein described.

Enquiring further into the source of economic power, as manifested by the achievements of men in the field of business, let us study the case of the Chicago group known as the Big Six, consisting of Wm. Wrigley, Jr., who owns the chewing gum business bearing his name, and whose individual income is said to be more than fifteen million dollars a year; John R. Thompson, who operates the chain of lunch rooms bearing his name; Mr. A. D. Lasker, who owns the Lord & Thomas Advertising Agency; Mr. McCullough, who owns the Parmalee Express Company, the largest transfer business in America; and, Mr. Ritchie and Mr. Hertz, who own the Yellow Taxicab business.

A reliable financial reporting company has estimated the yearly income of these six men at upward of twenty-five million dollars ($25,000,000), or an average of more than four million dollars a year per man.

Analysis of the entire group of six men discloses the fact that not one of them had any special educational advantages; that all began without capital or extensive credit; that their financial achievement has been due to their own individual plans and not to any fortunate turn of the wheel of chance.

Many years ago these six men formed a friendly alliance, meeting at stated periods for the purpose of assisting one another with ideas and suggestions in their various and sundry lines of business endeavor.

With the exception of Hertz and Ritchie, none of the six men were in any manner associated in a legal partnership. These meetings were strictly for the purpose of co-operating on the give-and-take basis of assisting one another with ideas and suggestions.

It is said that each of the individuals belonging to this Big Six group is a millionaire many times over. As a rule there is nothing worthy of special comment on behalf of a man who does nothing more than accumulate a few million dollars. However, there is something connected with the financial success of this particular group of men that is well worth comment, study, analysis, and even emulation, and that "something" is the fact that they have learned how to coordinate their individual minds by blending them in a spirit of perfect harmony, thereby creating a "Master Mind" that unlocks, to each individual of the group, doors which are closed to most of the human race.

The United States Steel Corporation is one of the strongest and most powerful industrial organizations in the world. The idea out of which this great industrial giant grew was born in the mind of Elbert H. Gary, a more or less commonplace lawyer, who was born and reared in a small Illinois town near Chicago.

Mr. Gary surrounded himself with a group of men whose minds he successfully blended in a spirit of perfect harmony, thereby creating the "Master Mind" which is the moving spirit of the great United States Steel Corporation.

Search where you will and wherever you find an outstanding success in business, finance, industry, or in any of the professions, you may be sure that back of the success is some individual who has applied the principle of mind chemistry through which a "Master Mind" has been created. These outstanding successes often appear to be the handiwork of but one person, but search closely and the other individuals whose minds have been co-ordinated with his own may be found. Remember that two or more persons may operate the principle of mind chemistry so as to create a "Master Mind."

Power (man power) is *organized knowledge, expressed through intelligent action!*

No effort can be said to be *organized* unless the individuals engaged in the effort co-ordinate their knowledge and energy in a spirit of perfect harmony. Lack of such harmonious co-ordination of effort is the main cause of practically every business failure.

An interesting experiment was conducted by this author in collaboration with the students of a well-known college. Each student was requested to write an essay on "How and Why Henry Ford Became Wealthy."

Each student was required to describe, as a part of his or her essay, what was believed to be the nature of Ford's real assets, of what these assets consisted in detail.

The majority of the students gathered financial statements and inventories of the Ford assets and used these as the basis of their estimates of Ford's wealth.

Included in these "sources of Ford's wealth" were such items as cash in banks, raw and finished materials in stock, real estate and buildings, good will, estimated at from ten to twenty-five per cent of the value of the material assets.

One student out of the entire group of several hundred, answered as follows:

"Henry Ford's assets consist, in the main, of two items, viz: (1) Working capital and raw and finished materials; (2) The knowledge, gained from experience, by Henry Ford himself, and the co-operation of a well-trained organization which understands how to apply this knowledge to best advantage from the Ford viewpoint. It is impossible to estimate, with anything approximating correctness, the actual dollars and cents value of either of these two groups of assets, but it is my opinion that their relative values are:

The organized knowledge of the Ford Organization	75%
The value of cash and physical assets of every nature, including raw and finished materials	25%

This author is of the opinion that this statement was not compiled by the young man whose name was signed to it, without the assistance of some very analytical and experienced mind or minds.

Unquestionably the biggest asset that Henry Ford has is his own brain. Next to this would come the brains of his immediate circle of associates, for it has been through co-ordination of these that the physical assets which he controls were accumulated.

Destroy every plant the Ford Motor Company owns; every piece of machinery; every ton of raw or finished material; every finished automobile, and every dollar on deposit in any bank, and Ford would still be the most powerful man, economically, on earth. His brains which have built the Ford business could duplicate it again in short order. Capital is always available in unlimited quantities, to such brains as Ford's.

Economically, Ford is the most powerful man on earth, because he has the keenest and most practical conception of the principle of *organized knowledge* of any man on earth, as far as this author has the means of knowing.

Despite Ford's great power and financial success, it may be that he has blundered often in the application of the principles through which he accumulated this power. There is but little doubt that Ford's methods of mind co-ordination have often been crude; they must needs have been in the earlier days of this experience, before he gained the wisdom of application that would naturally go with maturity of years.

Neither can there be but little doubt that Ford's application of the principle of mind chemistry was, at least at the start, the result of a chance alliance with other minds; particularly the mind of Edison. It is more than probable that Mr. Ford's remarkable insight into the law of nature was first begun as the result of his friendly alliance with his own wife long before he ever met either Mr. Edison or Mr. Firestone. Many a man is made by his wife, through application of the "Master Mind" principle, who never knows the real source of his success. Mrs. Ford is a most remarkably intelligent woman, and this author has reason to believe that it was her mind, blended with Mr. Ford's, which gave him his first real start toward power.

It may be mentioned, without in any way depriving Ford of any honor or glory, that in his earlier days he had to combat the powerful enemies of illiteracy and ignorance to a greater extent than did either Edison or Firestone, both of whom were gifted by natural heredity with a most fortunate aptitude for acquiring and applying knowledge. Ford had to hew his talent out of the rough, raw timbers of his none too favorable hereditary estate.

Within an inconceivably short period of time Ford has mastered three of the most stubborn enemies of mankind and transformed them into assets constituting the very foundation of his success.

These enemies are: Ignorance, illiteracy, and poverty!

Any man who can stay the hand of these three savage forces, much less harness and use them to good account, is well worth close study by the less fortunate individuals.

This is an age of *industrial power* in which we are living!

The source of all this *power* is *organized effort*. Not only has the management of industrial enterprises efficiently organized individual workers, but in many instances mergers of industry have been affected in such a manner and to the end that these combinations (as in the case of the United States Steel Corporation, for example) have accumulated practically unlimited power.

One may hardly glance at the news of a day's events without seeing a report of some business, industrial, or financial merger, bringing under one management enormous resources and thus creating great power.

One day it is a group of banks; another day it is a chain of railroads; the next day it is a combination of steel plants, all merging, for the purpose of developing power through highly organized and coordinated effort.

Knowledge, general in nature and unorganized, is not *power*; it is only potential power—the material out of which real power may be developed. Any modern library contains an unorganized record of all the knowledge of value to which the present civilization is heir, but this knowledge is not power because it is not organized.

Every form of energy and every species of animal or plant life, to survive, must be organized. The oversized animals whose bones have filled Nature's bone yard through extinction have left mute, but certain evidence that non-organization means annihilation.

From the electron—the smallest particle of matter— to the largest star in the universe, these and every material thing in between these two extremes, offer proof positive that one of Nature's first laws is that of *organization*. Fortunate is the individual who recognizes the importance of this law and makes it his business to familiarize himself with the various ways in which the law may be applied to advantage.

The astute business man has not only recognized the importance of the law of organized effort, but he has made this law the warp and woof of his *power*.

Without any knowledge whatsover of the principle of mind chemistry, or that such a principle exists, many men have accumulated great power by merely organizing the knowledge they possessed. The majority of all who have discovered the principle of mind chemistry and developed that principle into a *"Master Mind"* have stumbled upon) this knowledge by the merest of accidents; often failing to recognize the real nature of their discovery or understand the source of their power.

This author is of the opinion that all living persons, who, at the present time, are consciously making use of the principle of mind chemistry in developing power

> The man who has a **DEFINITE AIM** in mind, and a definite plan for attaining it, has already gone nine-tenths of the way toward success.

through the blending of minds, may be counted on the fingers of the two hands, with, perhaps, several fingers left to spare.

If this estimate is even approximately true, the student will readily see that there is but slight danger of the field of mind chemistry practice becoming overcrowded.

It is a well-known fact that one of the most difficult tasks that any business man must perform is that of inducing those who are associated with him to coordinate their efforts in a spirit of harmony. To induce continuous co-operation between a group of workers in any undertaking is next to impossible. Only the most efficient leaders can accomplish this highly desired object, but once in a great while such a leader will rise above the horizon in the field of industry, business, or finance, and then the world hears of a Henry Ford, Thomas A. Edison, John D. Rockefeller, Sr., E. H. Harriman, or James J. Hill.

Power and success are synonymous terms!

One grows out of the other; therefore, any person who has the knowledge and the ability to develop power, through the principle of harmonious co-ordination of effort between individual minds, or in any other manner, may be successful in any reasonable undertaking that is possible of successful termination.

It must not be presumed that a "Master Mind" will immediately spring, mushroom fashion, out of every group of minds which make a pretense of co-ordination in a spirit of *harmony!*

Harmony, in the real sense of meaning of the word, is as rare among groups of people as is genuine Christianity among those who proclaim themselves Christians.

Harmony is the nucleus around which the state of mind known as the "Master Mind" must be developed. Without this element of harmony there can be no "Master Mind," a truth which cannot be repeated too often.

Woodrow Wilson had in mind the development of a "Master Mind," to be composed of minds representing the civilized nations of the world, in his proposal of the League of Nations. Wilson's conception was the most far-reaching humanitarian idea ever created in the mind of man, because it dealt with a principle which embraces sufficient power to establish a real Brotherhood of Man on earth. The League of Nations, or some similar blending of international minds, in a spirit of harmony, is sure to become a reality.

The time when such unity of minds will take place will be measured largely by the time required for the great universities and *nonsectarian* institutions of learning to supplant ignorance and superstition with understanding and wisdom. This time is rapidly approaching.

The Psychology of the Revival Meeting

The old religious orgy known as the "revival" offers a favorable opportunity to study the principle of mind chemistry known as "Master Mind."

It will be observed that music plays no small part in bringing about the harmony essential to the blending of a group of minds in a revival meeting. Without music the revival meeting would be a tame affair.

During revival services the leader of the meeting has no difficulty in creating harmony in the minds of his devotees, but it is a well-known fact that this state of harmony lasts no longer than the presence of the leader, after which the "Master Mind" he has temporarily created, disintegrates.

By arousing the emotional nature of his followers, the revivalist has no difficulty, under the proper stage setting and with the embellishment of the right sort of music, in creating a "Master Mind" which becomes noticeable to all who come in contact with it. The very air becomes charged with a positive, pleasing influence which changes the entire chemistry of all minds present.

The revivalist calls this energy the "Spirit of the Lord."

This author, through experiments conducted with a group of scientific investigators and laymen, who were unaware of the nature of the experiment, has created the same state of mind and the same positive atmosphere without calling it the "Spirit of the Lord."

On many occasions this author has witnessed the creation of the same positive atmosphere in a group of men and women engaged in the business of salesmanship, without calling it the "Spirit of the Lord."

The author helped conduct a school of salesmanship for Harrison Parker, founder of the Co-operative Society, of Chicago, and, by the use of the same principle of mind chemistry, which the revivalist calls the "Spirit of the Lord," so transformed the nature of a group of 3,000 men and women (all of them were without former sales experience) that they sold more than $10,000,000 worth of securities in less than nine months, and earned more than one million dollars for themselves.

It was found that the average person who joined this school would reach the zenith of his or her selling power within one week, after which it was necessary to revitalize the individual's brain through a group sales meeting. These sales meetings were conducted on very much the same order as are the modern revival meetings of the religionists, with much the same stage equipment, including music and "high-powered" speakers, who exhorted the sales people in very much the same manner as does the modern religious revivalist.

Call it psychology, mind chemistry, or anything you please (they are all based upon the same principle), but there is nothing more certain than the fact that wherever a group of minds are brought into contact, in a spirit of *perfect harmony*, each mind in the group becomes immediately supplemented and re-enforced by a noticeable energy called a "Master Mind."

For all this writer professes to know, this uncharted energy may be the "Spirit of the Lord," but it operates just as favorably when called by any other name.

The human brain and nervous system constitute a piece of intricate machinery which but few, if any, understand. When controlled and properly directed, this piece of machinery can be made to perform wonders of achievement and, if not controlled, it will perform wonders fantastic and phantom-like in nature, as may be seen by examining the inmates of any insane asylum.

The human brain has direct connection with a continuous influx of energy from which man derives his power to think. The brain receives this energy, mixes it with the energy created by the food taken into the body, and distributes it to every portion of the body, through the aid of the blood and the nervous system. It thus becomes what we call life.

From what source this outside energy comes no one seems to know; all we know about it is that we must have it or die. It seems reasonable to presume that this energy is none other than that which we call ether, and, that it flows into the body along with the oxygen from the air, as we breathe.

Every normal human body possesses a first-class chemical laboratory and a stock of chemicals sufficient to carry on the business of breaking up, assimilating, and properly mixing and compounding the food we take into the body, preparatory to distributing it to wherever it is needed as a body builder.

Ample tests have been made, both with man and beast, to prove that the energy known as the mind plays an important part in this chemical operation of compounding and transforming of food into the required substances to build and keep the body in repair.

It is known that worry, excitement, or fear will interfere with the digestive process, and in extreme cases stop this process altogether, resulting in illness or death. It is obvious, then, that the mind enters into the chemistry of food digestion and distribution.

It is believed by many eminent authorities, although it may never have been scientifically proved, that the energy known as thought may become contaminated with negative or "unsociable" units to such an extent that the whole nervous system is thrown out of working order, digestion is interfered with, and various and sundry forms of disease will manifest themselves. Financial difficulties and unrequited love affairs head the list of causes of such mind disturbances.

A negative environment, such as that existing where some member of the family is constantly "nagging," will interfere with the chemistry of the mind to such an extent that the individual will lose ambition and gradually sink into oblivion. It is because of this fact that the old saying that a man's wife may either "make" or "break" him is literally true.

Any high school student knows that certain food combinations will, if taken into the stomach, result in indigestion, violent pain, and even death. Good health depends, in part at least, upon a food combination that "harmonizes." But harmony of food combination is not sufficient to insure good health; there must be harmony also between the units of energy known as the mind.

"Harmony" is one of Nature's laws, without which there can be no such thing as *organized energy,* or life in any form whatsoever.

The health of the body as well as the mind, is literally built upon the principle of *harmony!* The energy known as life begins to disintegrate and death approaches when the organs of the body stop working in harmony.

The moment harmony ceases at the source of any form of organized energy (power), units of that energy are thrown into a chaotic state of disorder and the power is rendered neutral or passive.

Harmony is also the nucleus around which the principle of mind chemistry known as a "Master Mind" develops power. Destroy this harmony and you destroy the power growing out of the co-ordinated effort of a group of individual minds.

This truth has been stated, restated, and presented in every manner which the author could conceive, with unending repetition, for the reason that unless the student grasps this principle and learns to apply it, this treatise on the Master Mind is useless.

Success in life, no matter what one may call success, is very largely a matter of adaptation to environment in such a manner that there is harmony between the individual and his environment. The palace of a king becomes as a hovel of a peasant if harmony does not abound within its walls. Conversely stated, the hut of a peasant may be made to yield more happiness than that of the mansion of the rich man, if harmony obtains in the former and not in the latter.

Without perfect harmony the science of astronomy would be as useless as the "bones of a saint," because the stars and planets would clash with one another, and all would be in a state of chaos and disorder.

Without the law of harmony the blood might deposit the food which grows finger nails, on the scalp where hair is supposed to grow, and thus create a horny growth which might easily be mistaken, by the superstitious, to signify man's relationship to a certain imaginary gentleman with horns often referred to by the more primitive type.

Without the law of harmony there can be no organization of knowledge, for what, may one ask, is organized knowledge except the harmony of facts and truths and natural laws?

The moment discord begins to creep in at the front door, harmony edges out at the back door, so to speak, whether the application is made to a business partnership or the orderly movement of the planets of the heavens.

If the student gathers the impression that the author is laying undue stress upon the importance of *harmony*, let it be remembered that lack of harmony is the first, and often the last and only cause of *failure!*

There can be no poetry, nor music, nor oratory worthy of notice without the presence of harmony.

Good architecture is largely a matter of harmony. Without harmony a house is nothing but a mass of building material, more or less a monstrosity.

Sound business management plants the very sinews of its existence in harmony.

Every well-dressed man or woman is a living picture and a moving example of harmony.

With all these "work-a-day" illustrations of the important part which harmony plays in the affairs of the world, nay, in operation of the entire universe, how could any intelligent person leave harmony out of his "Definite Aim" in life? As well have no "Definite Aim" as to omit harmony as the chief stone of its foundation.

———————

The human body is a complex organization of organs, glands, blood vessels, nerves, brain cells, muscles, etc. The mind energy which stimulates to action and co-ordinates the efforts of the component parts of the body is also a plurality of ever-varying and changing energies. From birth until death there is a continuous struggle, often assuming the nature of open combat, between the forces of the mind. For example, the lifelong struggle between the motivating forces and desires of the human mind, which take place between the impulses of right and wrong, are well known to everyone.

Every human being possesses at least two distinct mind powers or personalities, and as many as six distinct personalities have been discovered in one person. One of man's most delicate tasks is that of harmonizing these mind forces so that they may be organized and directed toward the orderly attainment of a given objective. Without this element of harmony no individual can become an accurate thinker.

It is no wonder that leaders in business and industrial enterprises, as well as those in other fields of endeavor, find it so difficult to organize groups of people so they will function without friction in the attainment of a given objective. Each individual human being possesses forces, within himself, which are hard to harmonize, even when he is placed in the environment most favorable to harmony. If the chemistry of the individual's mind is such that the units of his mind cannot be easily harmonized, think how much more difficult it must be to harmonize a group of minds so they will function as one, in an orderly manner, through what is known as a "Master Mind."

The leader who successfully develops and directs the energies of a "Master Mind" must possess tact, patience, persistence, self-confidence, intimate knowledge of mind chemistry, and the ability to adapt himself (in a state of perfect poise and harmony) to quickly changing circumstances without showing the least sign of annoyance.

How many are there who can measure up to this requirement?

The successful leader must possess the ability to change the color of his mind, Chameleon-like, to fit every circumstance that arises in connection with the object of his leadership. Moreover, he must possess the ability to change from one mood to another without showing the slightest signs of anger or lack of self-control. The successful leader must understand the Seventeen Laws of

Success and be able to put into practice any combination of these laws whenever occasion demands.

Without this ability no leader can be powerful, and without power no leader can long endure.

The Meaning of Education

There has long been a general misconception of the meaning of the word "educate." The dictionaries have not aided in the elimination of this misunderstanding because they have defined the word "educate" as an act of imparting knowledge.

The word educate has its roots in the Latin word *educo*, which means to develop *from within;* to educe; to draw out; to grow through the law of *use.*

Nature hates idleness in all its forms. She gives continuous life only to those elements which are in use. Tie up an arm, or any other portion of the body, taking it out of use, and the idle part will soon atrophy and become lifeless. Reverse the order, give an arm more than normal use, such as that engaged in by the blacksmith who wields a heavy hammer all day long, and that arm (developed from within) grows strong.

Power grows out of *organized knowledge,* but, mind you, it "grows out of it" through application and use!

A man may become a walking encyclopedia of knowledge without possessing any power of value. This knowledge becomes power only to the extent that it is organized, classified and put into action. Some of the best educated men the world has known possessed much less general knowledge than some who have been known as fools, the difference between the two being that the former put what knowledge they possessed into use, while the latter made no such application.

An "educated" person is one who knows how to acquire everything he needs in the attainment of his main purpose in, life, without violating the rights of his fellow men. It might be a surprise to many so-called men of "learning" to know that they come nowhere near qualification as men of "education." It might also be a great surprise to many who believe they suffer from lack of "learning" to know that they are well "educated."

The successful lawyer is not necessarily the one who memorizes the greatest number of principles of law. On the contrary, the successful lawyer is the one who knows where to find a principle of law, plus a variety of opinions supporting that principle which fit the immediate needs of a given case.

In other words, the successful lawyer is he who knows where to find the law he wants when he needs it.

This principle applies, with equal force, to the affairs of industry and business.

Henry Ford had but little elementary schooling, yet he is one of the best "educated" men in the world because he has acquired the ability to so combine natural and economic laws, to say nothing of the minds of men, that he has the power to get anything of a material nature he wants.

Some years ago during the World War, Mr. Ford brought suit against the *Chicago Tribune*, charging that newspaper with libelous publication of statements concerning him, one of which was the statement that Ford was an "ignoramus," an ignorant pacifist, etc.

When the suit came up for trial, the attorneys for *the Tribune* undertook to prove, by Ford himself, that their statement was true; that he was ignorant, and with this object in view they catechized and cross-examined him on all manner of subjects.

One question they asked was:

"How many soldiers did the British send over to subdue the rebellion in the Colonies in 1776?"

With a dry grin on his face Ford nonchalantly replied:

"I do not know just how many, but I have heard that it was a lot more than ever went back."

Loud laughter from Court, jury, court room spectators, and even from the frustrated lawyer who had asked the question.

This line of interrogation was continued for an hour or more, Ford remaining perfectly calm the meanwhile. Finally, however, he had permitted the "smart Aleck" lawyers to play with him until he was tired of it, and in reply to a question which was particularly obnoxious and insulting, Ford straightened himself up, pointed his finger at the questioning lawyer and replied:

"If I should really wish to answer the foolish questions you have just asked, or any of the others you have been asking, let me remind you that I have a row of electric push buttons hanging over my desk and, by placing my finger on the right button, I could call in men who could give me the correct answer to all the questions you have asked and to many that you have not the intelligence to either ask or answer. Now, will you kindly tell me why I should bother about filling my mind with a lot of useless details in order to answer every fool question that anyone may ask, when I have able men all about me who can supply me with all the facts I want when I call for them?"

This answer is quoted from memory, but it substantially relates Ford's answer.

There was silence in the court room. The questioning attorney's underjaw dropped down, his eyes opened widely; the judge leaned forward from the bench and gazed in Mr. Ford's direction; many of the jury awoke and looked around as if they had heard an explosion, which they actually had.

A prominent clergyman, who was present in the court room at the time, said later that the scene reminded him of that which must have existed when Jesus Christ was on trial before Pontius Pilate, just after he had given his famous reply to Pilate's question, "What is truth?"

In the vernacular of the day, Ford's reply knocked the questioner cold.

Up to the time of that reply the lawyer had been enjoying considerable fun at what he believed to be Ford's expense, by adroitly displaying his (the lawyer's) sample case of general knowledge and comparing it with what he inferred to be Ford's ignorance as to many events and subjects.

But that answer spoiled the lawyer's fun!

It also proved once more (to all who had the intelligence to accept the proof) that true education means mind development; not merely the gathering and classifying of knowledge.

Ford could not, in all probability, have named the capitals of all the States of the United States, but he could have, and in fact had, gathered the "capital" with which to "turn many wheels" within every state in the Union.

Education—let us not forget this—consists of the power with which to get everything one needs without violating the rights of his fellow men. Ford comes well within that definition, for the reason which the author has here tried to make plain, by relating the foregoing incident connected with the simple Ford philosophy.

There are many men of "learning" who could easily entangle Ford, theoretically, with a maze of questions none of which he, personally, could answer. But Ford could wage a battle in industry or finance that would exterminate those same men with all of their abstract knowledge and wisdom.

> Education consists of doing—not merely of KNOWING!

Ford probably could not go into his chemical laboratory and separate water into its component atoms of hydrogen and oxygen and then recombine these atoms in their former order, but he knows how to surround himself with chemists who can do this for him if he wants it done. *The man who can intelligently use the knowledge possessed by another is as much or more a man of education as the person who merely has the knowledge but does not know what to do with it.*

The Relationship between Sexual Urge and Genius

The urge of sex is, by far, the most powerful of the eight basic motivating forces which stimulate the mind to *action*. Because of the importance of this subject it has been reserved as the closing chapter of the first of the seventeen factors constituting the Law of Success.

The part which sexual urge plays in the achievement of outstanding success was first discovered by the author in his studies of the biographies of great leaders, and in his analysis of men and women of the present age who have risen high in their chosen fields of endeavor.

The subject of sex is one in connection with which most people are unpardonably ignorant. Sexual urge has been slandered and burlesqued by the ignorant and the vulgar-minded for so long that the very word sex is seldom mentioned in polite society. Men and women who are known to be blessed with highly sexed natures are usually looked upon as people who will bear watching, and, instead of being called "blessed," they are usually called "cursed."

During the early years of research, when this philosophy was in the embryonic stage, the author made the discovery that every great leader in art and music, and literary work and statesmanship, and in practically every other walk of life, was a highly sexed person. Among the group whose biographies were carefully studied let us mention, for the purpose of refreshing the reader's memory on the subject, the following:

Napoleon Bonaparte   Ralph Waldo Emerson

Shakespeare   Robert Burns

George Washington   Thomas Jefferson

Abraham Lincoln

Let us recall, also, a few names of highly sexed gentlemen of a later age who are known to have been men of great achievement in their respective callings:

Elbert Hubbard   Oscar Wilde

Elbert H. Gary   Woodrow Wilson

John H. Patterson   Enrico Caruso
Stanford White

For ethical reasons it would hardly be appropriate to mention the names of men who are still living, but the reader may easily supply these names by taking inventory of *all* men who enjoy the reputation of great leadership in their respective callings.

Sexual urge is the highest and most refined form of human emotion. It "steps up" the rate of vibration of the mind as no other emotion can, and causes the imaginative faculties of the brain to function in the form of *genius*. Far from being something of which one should be ashamed, a highly sexed nature is a blessing of which one should feel proud, and for which no apologies should be offered.

The Value of Transmutation of Sexual Urge

To be highly sexed is not sufficient, of itself, to produce a genius. Only those who understand the nature of sexual urge, and who know how to transmute this powerful emotion into other channels of action than that of sexual contact, rise to the status of a genius. The urge of sex is a driving force compared to which all other motivating forces must take second place at best. A mind that has been aroused through intense sexual desire becomes receptive to the impulse of ideas which "flash" into the mind from outside sources through what is ordinarily known as *inspiration*.

It is the belief of this author—a belief not without considerable evidence to back it—that all so-called "revelations," of whatever nature, from religion to art, are superinduced by intense desire for sexual contact. All so-called "magnetic" people are highly sexed. People who are brilliant, charming, versatile, and accomplished are generally highly sexed. Prove this for yourself by analyzing those whom you know to be highly sexed.

Destroy the capacity for strong sexual desire and you have removed all that is powerful about a human being. If you wish proof of this, observe what happens to the "spirited" stallion or any other male animal, such as a bull or a hog, after it has been altered sexually; the moment sexual urge has been destroyed in any animal, from man on down to the lowest forms of animal life, the capacity for dominating *action* goes with it. This is a statement of biological fact too well known to be disputed. Moreover, it is a fact that is significant, and important.

Sex Energy Has Therapeutic Value

It is a fact well known to scientists, although not generally known to the layman, that sexual contact has a therapeutic value unknown in connection with any other human emotion. This fact may be easily verified, however, by even the most casual study of the subject, by observing the physical state of the body following sexual contact between two people who are properly mated or affinitized. What mind is so vulgar and ignorant as not to have observed that following sexual contact, between two people who are properly "balanced," or mated, the physical body becomes relaxed and calm? Relaxation, superinduced in this manner, provides the nervous system with a most favorable opportunity to balance and distribute the nervous energy of the body to all the organs of the body. *Properly distributed nervous energy is the force which maintains a healthy body.* Also, nervous energy properly distributed, through relaxation, is the agency which eliminates the cause of all physical ailments.

These briefly stated facts are not mere opinions of the author of this philosophy. They have been gleaned from twenty-five years of careful research in connection with which the author has had the collaboration of some of the most eminent scientists known to the past and present generation, one of whom was a well-known physician who was bold enough to admit that he had often recommended a change in sexual consorts for patients who were suffering from hypochondriacal conditions (patients suffering with imaginary illness), and in that manner produced cures that would not have been possible in any other manner. This physician went even farther by predicting that the time was not far distant when this form of therapeutics would be more generally understood and used. The suggestion is here offered for what it may be worth, without comment from the author of this philosophy other than the statement that most of the human race is still woefully ignorant of the possibilities of the urge of sex, not only in connection with the maintenance of health, but also in connection with the creation of genius.

It seemed quite significant to this author, when he made the discovery that practically every great leader, whom he has had the privilege of studying at close range, was a man whose achievements were largely inspired by a woman. In many instances, the "woman in the case" is a modest little wife of whom the public hears but little. In a few cases the source of inspiration has been traced to the "other woman." A great, enduring love is a sufficient motive to drive even a mediocre man to unbelievable heights of achievement, a statement of fact which should be kept in mind by all wives of men.

Sexual urge is the most effective known agency through which the mind may be "stepped up" to where it becomes a Master Mind!

The Ten Major Sources of Mind Stimulation

It may be helpful to here outline the major sources of mind stimulation, in view of the fact that all great achievements are the result of some form of stimuli which "step up" the mind to a high rate of vibration. These stimuli are listed in the order of what the author believes to be their importance, as follows:

1. *Sexual contact* between two people who are motivated by a genuine feeling of love.
2. *Love,* not necessarily accompanied by sexual contact.
3. *Burning desire* for fame, power, and financial gain.
4. *Music.* Acts as a mighty stimulant to a highly emotionalized person.
5. *Friendship,* between either those of the same sex or the opposite sex, accompanied by a desire to be mutually helpful in some definite undertaking or calling.
6. *Master Mind alliance,* between two or more people who ally themselves, mentally, for the purpose of mutual help, in a spirit of unselfishness.
7. *Mutual suffering,* such as that experienced by people who are unjustly persecuted, through racial, religious, and economic differences of opinion.
8. *Autosuggestion,* through which an individual may step up his or her own mind, through constant self-suggestion with a definite motive. (Perhaps this source of mind stimulation should have been placed nearer the top of the list).
9. *Suggestion.* The influence of outside suggestion may lift one to great heights of achievement, or, if negatively used, dash one to the bottomless pit of failure and destruction.

10. *Narcotics and alcohol.* This source of mind stimulation is totally destructive, and leads, finally, to negation of all the other nine sources of stimulation.

Mind stimulant is any influence which will, temporarily or permanently, "step up" the rate of vibration of the brain. Here you have a brief description of all the major sources of mind stimulation. Through these sources of stimulation one may commune, temporarily, with Infinite Intelligence, a procedure which constitutes all there is of genius. *The forgeoing statement is definite and plain. Take it or leave it, just as you please!* The statement is made as a positive fact because this author has had the privilege of helping to raise scores of mediocre men and women out of mediocrity into states of mind which entitled them to rank as geniuses. Some have been able to remain in this exalted state, while others have relapsed to their former status, either temporarily or permanently.

The author personally interviews and analyzes an average of a dozen men and women every day for the purpose of helping them discover the most suitable source of mind stimulation and the most profitable outlet for their talent resulting from this stimulation.

On many scores of occasions the author has had the experience of seeing a client create some useful invention, or some unique plan of rendering useful service, right in the midst of the analysis.

Not two hours previous to the writing of these lines a client whose name is H. Gundelach came, with his wife, for analysis, and before the work had proceeded for more than thirty minutes, Mr. Gundelach conceived an idea for a new style of interlocking brick suitable for building public highways which has the possibility of rendering useful service all over America, to say nothing of making a huge fortune for himself. Perhaps it would be more correct to say that the three of us— he and his wife and the author—conceived the idea simultaneously.

Intemperance

The use of alcohol and narcotics as mind stimulants is condemned without exception, on the ground that such use eventually destroys the normal functioning power of the brain. While it is true that some of the greatest literary geniuses of the past used liquor as a mind stimulant, with temporary success, it is equally true that such use generally became an excess which destroyed them. Edgar Allan Poe and Robert Burns both used alcohol as a mind stimulant, with telling effects, but both were finally destroyed through *excessive* use of this form of stimulant. Of the ten stimulants described in this chapter, but nine are safe for use and even these cannot be used excessively.

Sexual contact is the most powerful of all the mind stimulants, but, this, too, may be used to excess with as damaging effects as the excessive use of alcohol or narcotics. Excessive eating may be just as damaging as any other form of excess, and in many thousands of cases this form of indulgence destroys all possibility of great achievement.

One of the seventeen factors of the Law of Success is that of self-control. As will be seen, when that subject is reached, self-control, in the sense that it is a part of this philosophy, is a balance wheel which guards the individual against excesses of every nature whatsoever. The three major excesses which are destroying people throughout the world to-day are: the excess of eating, the excess of sexual indulgence, and the excess of strong drinks and drugs. *One is just as fatal to success as either of the other two.*

Why Men Do Not Succeed Before Forty

The major reason why the average man does not begin to strike his real stride in his chosen life work, before the age of forty, *is his tendency to dissipate his energy through overindulgence in sexual contact*. The average male does not learn that sexual urge has other possibilities than that of use in sexual contact, until he has reached the age of forty to forty-five years. Up to this age the life of the average male (in which classification the majority of all males may be properly placed) is just one long, continuous orgy of sexual intercourse, through which all his finer and more powerful emotions are sown wildly to the four winds. This is not merely the opinion of this author; it is a statement of fact based upon careful analysis of over twenty thousand people. Intelligent study and analysis of twenty thousand people gives a very accurate cross-section classification of the entire human race.

Between overeating and overindulgence in sexual contact, the average man has but little energy left for other uses, until he has passed the age of forty, and in altogether too many instances men never gain mastery of themselves with reference to these two forms of weakness. A sad statement of fact is the truth that the majority of men do not look upon overindulgence in eating and in sexual contact as being dangerous excesses which destroy their chances of success in life. There is no argument over the detrimental effects of excessive use of alcohol and narcotics, as everyone knows that such overindulgence is fatal to success, but not everyone knows that excesses in sexual contact and in eating can be just as ruinous.

The desire for sexual contact is the strongest, most powerful, and most impelling of all human desires, and for this very reason it may be harnessed and transmuted into channels other than that of sexual tact in a manner that will raise one to great heights of genius. On the other hand, this powerful urge, if not controlled and so transmuted, may and often does lower man to the level of an ordinary beast.

In closing this chapter, may the author not offer a word of reply to those who may feel that even the very brief reference here made to the subject of sex might be harmful to the young men and young women? The reply is this: *Ignorance of the subject of sex, due to lack of free discussion of the subject by those who really understand it, has resulted in destructive use of the emotion of sex all back down the ages.* Moreover, if anyone should feel that this brief reference might hurt the morals of the young people of this generation, let that person keep in mind the fact that most young people get their sex education from less commendable sources than a book of this nature, and such education is generally accompanied by interpretations of the power of sex which in no way relate the subjects of sex and genius, and in no manner even suggest that there is such a possibility as the transmutation of sex power into art and literary works of the most commendable order, and business leadership, and a multitude of other constructive forms of helpful service. This is an age of frank discussion of the great mysteries of life, among which the subject of sex may be properly classified. Finally, the urge of sex is biological in nature and *it cannot be suppressed through silence!* In truth, the emotion of sexual urge is the finest of all human emotions, and the sexual relationship the most beautiful of all relationships. Why, then, cast the slurring innuendo that the sexual relationship is something ugly and vulgar by trying to shroud the subject in a dark background of silence?

———————

For lack of space the subject of the Master Mind must be ended here. We pass next to the discussion of the second of the seventeen factors of the Law of Success, with both apology and regret that this lack of space forbids us to discuss the remaining sixteen subjects as extensively as we have covered the subject of the Master Mind.

LESSON TWO

A Definite Chief Aim

To be successful in any sort of endeavor you must have a *definite* goal toward which to work. You must have definite plans for attaining this goal. Nothing is ever accomplished that is worthwhile without a definite plan of procedure that is systematically and continuously followed out day by day.

A definite chief aim is placed at the beginning of the Seventeen Laws of Success for the reason that without it the other Sixteen Laws would be useless, for how could one hope to succeed, or how could one know when he had succeeded, without first having determined what he wanted to accomplish?

During the past twenty odd years the author has analyzed more than twenty thousand people, in nearly all walks of life, and startling as it may seem, ninety-five per cent of these people were failures. By this is meant that they were barely making enough on which to exist, some of them not even doing this well. The other five per cent were successful, meaning by *"success"* that they were making enough for all their needs and laying something by for the sake of ultimate financial independence.

Now the significant thing about this discovery was that the five per cent who were succeeding had *a definite chief aim* and also a plan for attaining that aim. In other words, those who knew what they wanted, and had a plan for getting it, were succeeding while those who did not know what they wanted were *getting just that—nothing!*

If a man is engaged in the business of selling, or rendering service which calls for methods of handling his customers that will cause them to patronize him continuously, he must have a *definite plan* for bringing about this result. The plan may be one thing, or it may be something else, but in the main it should be distinctive and of such a nature that it will impress itself upon the minds of his patrons in a *favorable* manner. Anyone can hand out merchandise to those who come, voluntarily, and ask for it, but not everyone has acquired the art of delivering with the merchandise that unseen "something" which causes the customer to repeat and come back for more. Here is where the necessity of a *definite aim* and a definite plan for attaining it enters.

Within recent years gasoline filling stations have become so numerous that one may be found just around the corner, so to speak, in every community. The gas, oil, and other supplies sold at the majority of these service stations is good, there being but little difference between the quality received at one station and that received at another. Despite this fact, however, there are motorists who will drive miles out of their way, or delay the purchase of oil and gas until the very last minute, for the purpose of buying these supplies from some "favorite" service station.

Now, the question arises, *"What causes these people to do this?"*

And the answer is, *"People trade at service stations where they are served by men who cultivate them."*

What is meant by *"men who cultivate them?"* It means that a few filling station men have created *definite plans* for studying and catering to motorists in such a manner that these motorists will return again. Good oil and gas, alone, cannot compete with the filling station manager who makes it his business to know people and cater to them according to their mannerisms and characteristics. One filling station manager makes it his business to watch the tires on every automobile that drives up, and when he sees a tire that needs more inflation he promptly "gives it the air." If the windshield is dusty or dirty he wipes it with a wet cloth. If a car is covered with dust he gets busy with a duster. In these and scores of other ways, he impresses the motorist with the fact that he makes it his business to render service that is a bit different. All this does not "just happen." He has a *definite plan* and also a *definite purpose* in doing it, and that purpose is to bring motorists back to his station.

This is a brief statement of what is meant by *a definite chief aim.*

Let us now go a bit deeper into the study of the psychological principle upon which the law of *a definite chief aim* is based. Careful study of more than one hundred of the leading men in practically all walks of life has disclosed the fact that every one of these men worked with *a definite chief aim* and also a *definite plan* for its attainment.

The human mind is something like a magnet in that it will attract the counterparts of the dominating thoughts held in the mind, and especially those which constitute *a definite chief aim* or purpose. For example, if a man establishes, as his *definite chief aim,* and as his daily working purpose, the adding of say one hundred new customers who will regularly purchase the merchandise or service he is rendering, immediately that aim or purpose becomes a dominating influence in his mind, and this influence will drive him to do that which is necessary to secure these additional one hundred customers.

Manufacturers of automobiles and other lines of merchandise often establish what they call "quotas," covering the number of automobiles or the amount of merchandise that must be sold in each territory. These "quotas," when definitely established, constitute a *definite chief aim* toward which all who are engaged in the distribution of the automobiles or merchandise direct their efforts. Seldom does anyone fail to make the established quotas, but it is a well-known fact that had there been no "quotas" the actual sales would have been far less than they were with them. In other words, to achieve success in selling or in practically any other line of endeavor, one must set up a mark at which to shoot, so to speak, and without this target there will be but slim results.

Scientists have discovered in recent years, along with the other startling discoveries such as radio, television, mastery of the air, etc., that any man may achieve practically any end which he may set up in his own mind as *a definite chief aim*. It is literally true that the man with a definite purpose, and with full faith in his ability to realize that purpose, cannot be permanently defeated. He may meet with temporary defeat; perhaps many such defeats, but *failure*, never!

Your first step on the road to Success is to know where you are going, how you intend to travel, and when you intend to get there, which is only another way of saying that you must determine upon *a definite chief aim*. This aim, when decided upon, must be written out in clear language so it can be understood by any other person. If there is anything "hazy" about your aim, it is not *definite*. A man who knew what he was saying once stated

> There is a sure way to avoid criticism; be nothing, do nothing! Get a job as street-sweeper and kill off ambition. The formula always works.

that nine-tenths of success, in any undertaking, was in knowing what was wanted. This is true.

The moment you write out a statement of your *chief aim,* your action plants an image of that aim firmly in your subconscious mind, and, through some process which even the most enlightened scientists have not yet discovered, Nature causes your subconscious mind to use that *chief aim* as a pattern or blue print by which the major portion of your thoughts, ideas, and efforts are directed toward the attainment of the objective on which the *aim* is based.

This is a strange, abstract truth—something that cannot be weighed, meditated upon—but it is a truth nevertheless!

You will be taken further into the mysteries of this strange law when you reach the law of *imagination,* further on, and also when you reach some of the other laws.

LESSON THREE

Self-Confidence

The third of the Seventeen Laws of Success is Self-Confidence. This term is self-explanatory—it means that to achieve success you must believe in yourself. However, this does not mean that you have no limitations; it means that you are to take inventory of yourself, find out what qualities you have that are strong and useful, and then organize these qualities into a *definite plan* of action with which to attain the object of your *definite chief aim*.

In all the languages of the world there is no one word that carries the same or even approximately the same meaning as the word "*faith*." If there are any such things as "miracles," they are performed only with the aid of super-faith. The doubting type of mind is not a creative mind. Search where and how you may, and you will not discover one single record of great achievement, in any line of endeavor, that was not conceived in *imagination* and brought into reality through

To succeed, you must have *faith* in your own ability to do whatever you make up your mind to do. Also, you must cultivate the habit of *faith* in those who are associated with you, whether they are in position of authority over you, or you over them. The psychological reason for this will be covered thoroughly and plainly in the Law on *Co-operation,* further on.

Doubters are not builders! Had Columbus lacked Self-Confidence and *faith* in his own judgment, the richest and most glorious spot of ground on this earth might never have been discovered, and these lines might never have been written. Had George Washington and his compatriots of the 1776 historical fame not possessed Self-Confidence, Cornwallis' armies would have conquered and the United States of America would be ruled to-day from a little island lying three thousand miles away in the East.

A definite chief aim is the starting point of all noteworthy achievement, but Self-Confidence is the unseen force which coaxes, drives, or leads one on and on until the object of the *aim* is a reality. Without Self-Confidence man's achievements would never get beyond the "aim" stage, and mere aims, within themselves, are worth nothing. Many people have vague sorts of aims, but they get nowhere because they lack the Self-Confidence to create *definite plans* for attaining these aims.

Fear is the main enemy of Self-Confidence. Every person comes into this world cursed, to some extent, with Six Basic Fears, all of which must be mastered before one may develop sufficient Self-Confidence to attain outstanding success.

These six basic fears are:

1. The Fear of Criticism
2. The Fear of Ill Health
3. The Fear of Poverty
4. The Fear of Old Age
5. The Fear of Loss of Love of Someone (ordinarily called jealousy)
6. The Fear of Death

Space will not permit a lengthy description of how and where these Six Fears came from. In the main, however, they were acquired through early childhood environment, by teaching, the telling of ghost stories, discussion of "hell-fire," and in many other ways. Fear of Criticism is placed at the head of the list because it is, perhaps, the most common and one of the most destructive of the entire six fears. But for the Fear of Criticism men would not have bald heads, because baldness is the result of tight hatbands, and hats are worn only because most men are afraid of what "they will say" if hats are left off. Women seldom have bald heads because they wear loose hats, permitting the nervous energy to properly feed the roots of the hair.

Knowledge of this basic Fear of Criticism brings hundreds of millions of dollars to the manufacturers of clothing each year, and costs timid people the same amount, because most people lack the personality or the courage to wear clothes which are one season out of style. To some extent this basic Fear of Criticism is employed by the manufacturers of automobiles who change models every season, as not many men wish to drive a car whose lines and general appearance are a season or so behind the times.

Before you can develop Self-Confidence sufficient to master the obstacles which stand between you and success, you must take inventory of yourself and find out how many of these six basic fears are standing in your way. A few days of study, thought, and reflection will readily enable you to lay your fingers on the particular fear or fears which stand between you and Self-Confidence. Once you discover these enemies, you may easily eliminate them, through procedure which will be described later on.

The fears of Ill Health, Poverty, Old Age and Death are mainly the results of the hold-over effects of teachings of a bygone age, when men were taught to believe that death might bring with it a world and a life more horrible than the one on this earth; a life associated with fire and eternal torment. The effect of this teaching so shocked the sensibilities of the human mind that fear became embedded in the subconscious mind and, in that manner, was transmitted from parent to child and thus kept alive from generation to generation. Scientists differ as to the extent that such fears can be transmitted from parent to child, through physical heredity, but they are all in accord on this point, that the discussion of such matters in the presence of a child is sufficient to plant the "*fear*" impulse in its subconscious mind, where nothing but strong resolution and great *faith* in a belief opposite to the thing feared can eliminate the damage done.

The Fear of Loss of Love of Someone (jealousy) is a hold over from the days of human savagery, when it was man's habit to steal his fellow man's mate by force. The practice of one man stealing another's mate still exists, to some extent, but the stealing is now done through allurements of one sort or another—fine clothes, motor cars, furs, jewels, and other trinkets—and not by the use of force. However, there is still enough of this element in the man animal to cause his fellow man to stand in awe of him, to some extent. Thus the Fear of Loss of Love (or jealousy) has a biological as well as an economic basis for its existence. Jealousy is a form of insanity, because it is often indulged in without the slightest reason for its existence. Despite this fact, this fear causes untold suffering, annoyance, and failure in this world. To understand the nature of this fear and how one comes by it is a step in the direction of its mastery.

Every student of this philosophy should do a certain amount of collateral reading, selecting biographies of men who have attained outstanding success, because this is sure to disclose the fact that these men met with practically every conceivable sort of temporary defeat, yet, despite these discouraging experiences, they developed Self-Confidence sufficient to enable them to master every obstacle that stood in their way. Among the books recommended by the author of the Law of Success are:

The Man From Maine, by Edward W. Bok
Compensation, by Ralph Waldo Emerson
The Age of Reason, by Thomas Paine
The Ascent of Man, by Henry Drummond
The Science of Power, by Benjamin Kidd

These five subjects will give you the complete story of the stupendously interesting evolutionary process through which the mind of man has reached its present stage of development. Incidentally, after reading these books, you will have a better basis on which to build Self-Confidence, for you will then understand why there are but few "impossibilities" known to man, if, in fact, there are any. By all means read the last two books if you cannot or do not wish to read the entire list. To do so, and to understand that which you read, will give you the equivalent of the best sort of college education from many viewpoints.

The Habit of Saving

It is an embarrassing admission, but it is true, that a poverty-stricken person is less than the dust of the earth as far as the achievement of noteworthy success is concerned. It may be, and perhaps is true, that *money is not success*, but unless you have it or can command its use, you will not get far, no matter what may be your *definite chief aim*. As business is conducted to-day—as civilization stands today—money is an absolute essential for success, and there is no known formula for financial independence except that which is connected, in one way or another, with systematic saving.

The amount saved from week to week or from month to month is not of great consequence so long as the saving is regular and systematic. This is true because the *habit* of saving adds something to the other qualities essential for success which can be had in no other way.

It is doubtful if any person can develop Self-Confidence to the highest possible point without the protection and independence which belong to those who have saved and are saving money. There is something about the knowledge that one has some money ahead which gives faith and self-reliance such as can be had in no other way.

Without money a person is at the mercy of every person who wishes to exploit or prey upon him. If the man who does not save and has no money offers his personal services for sale he must accept what the purchaser offers; there is no alternative.

If opportunity to profit by trade or otherwise comes along, it is of no avail to the man who has neither money nor credit, and it must be kept in mind that credit is generally based upon the money one has or its equivalent.

When the Law of Success philosophy was first created, the Law of Saving was not included as one of the Seventeen Laws, with the result that thousands of people who experimented with this philosophy found that it carried them almost within reach of their goal of success, only to dash their hopes to pieces on the rocks of—what? For years the author of the course and the creator of the philosophy searched for the reason why the philosophy fell just barely short of its intended purpose. Through many years of experimentation and research it was finally discovered that one Law was lacking, and that was the law of *the habit of saving.*

When this Law was added the students of the Law of Success philosophy began to prosper without exception, and now, barely three years since the discovery was made, thousands of people have used the philosophy for the attainment of success and not one single case of failure has been reported.

The amount of your income is of but little importance if you do not systematically save a portion of it. Ten thousand dollars a year income is no better than two thousand dollars unless a part of it is saved. As a matter of fact a ten-thousand-dollar-a-year income may be far worse for the man who received it than would be a two-thousand-dollar income, if the entire amount is spent and dissipated, because the act of dissipation may undermine the health and in other ways destroy the chances of success.

Millions of people have read stories by great writers of Henry Ford's stupendous achievements, and of his great wealth, but it is safe to say that not one out of every thousand of these people have taken the trouble or done enough thinking to determine the real basis of Ford's success. Through a test made by the author of the Law of Success philosophy, five hundred people were given an outline of the twelve fundamentals which have been largely responsible for Ford's success. In this outline it was pointed out that the amount of cash received each year from the floor sweepings and trash taken from the Ford plants amounts to nearly $600,000. Not one of the entire five hundred placed any significance upon this fact. Not one of the five hundred discovered, or if they did they failed to mention it, the fact that Ford has always been a systematic saver of resources.

The Spending *habit* is highly developed in most Americans, but we know little of the more important *habit* of saving. Woolworth built the highest skyscraper in the world and accumulated a fortune of over one hundred million dollars by *saving* the dimes which millions of Americans threw away for trash which they did not really need. The habit of spending money is a mama with most people, and this habit keeps their noses to the grindstone all the days of their fives.

Tests have been made which show, conclusively, that the majority of business men will not place their resources or even positions involving responsibilities in other directions in the hands of those who have not formed the habit of saving money. The *savings habit* is the finest sort of recommendation of any man, no matter what position he may hold or what position he may seek to hold.

The late James J. Hill (who was well prepared to speak with authority on the subject) said that there is a rule by which any man may test himself and determine, well in advance, whether or not he would succeed in life, and that this rule was, "He must have formed the habit of systematic saving of money."

Initiative and Leadership

All people may be placed in one or the other of two general classes. One is known as leaders and the other as followers. Not often do the "followers" achieve note-worthy success, and never succeed until they break away from the ranks of the "followers" and become "leaders."

There is a mistaken notion being broadcast in the world among a certain class of people, to the effect that a man is paid for that which he knows. This is only partly true, and, like all other half truths, it does more damage than an out-and-out falsehood.

The truth is that a man is paid not only for that which he *knows*, but more particularly for that which *he does* with what he knows, or, that which he *gets others to do*.

Without *initiative* no man will achieve success, no matter what he may consider success, because he will do nothing out of the ordinary run of mediocre work such as nearly all men are forced to do in order to have a place to sleep, something to eat, and clothes to wear. These three necessities may be had, of a certain kind, without the aid of *initiative* and *leadership*, but the moment a man makes up his mind to acquire more than the bare necessities of life, he must either cultivate the habits of *initiative* and *leadership* or else find himself hedged in behind a stone wall.

The first step essential in the development of *initiative* and *leadership* is that of forming the habit of prompt and firm *decision*. All successful people have a certain amount of *decision*. The man who wavers between two or more half-baked and more or less vague notions of what he wants to do generally ends by doing nothing.

There had been "talk" about building the Panama Canal for many generations, but the actual work of building the canal never got much beyond the "talk" stage until the late Theodore Roosevelt became President of the United States. With the firmness of *decision* which was the very warp and woof of his achievements and the real basis of his reputation as a leader, Roosevelt took the *initiative*, had a bill framed for Congress to pass, providing the money, went to work with a spirit of *self-confidence*, plus a *definite chief aim* and a *definite plan* for its attainment, and lo! the much-talked-of Panama Canal became a splendid reality.

It is not enough to have a *definite chief aim* and a *definite plan* for its achievement, even though the plan may be perfectly practical and you may have all the necessary ability to carry it through successfully—you must have more than these—you must actually take the *initiative* and put the wheels of your plan into motion and keep them turning until your goal has been reached.

Study those whom you know to be failures (you'll find them all around you) and observe that, without a single exception, they lack the firmness of *decision,* even in matters of the smallest importance. Such people usually "talk" a great deal, but they are very short on performance. "Deeds, not words" should be the motto of the man who intends to succeed in life, no matter what may be his calling, or what he has selected as his *definite chief aim.*

Lack of *decision* has often resulted in insanity. Nothing is very bad or dreadful, once one has reached a decision to face the consequences. This truth was demonstrated quite effectively by a man who was condemned to die in the electric chair. When asked how it felt to know that he was to die in another half hour he replied, "Well, it does not bother me in the least. I made up my mind that I had to go sometime, and it might as well be now as a few years later, because my life has been nothing but a sad failure and a constant source of trouble anyway. Just think, it will soon all be over!"

The man was actually relieved to know that the responsibilities of life to which he had been subjected, and which had brought him to such an ignoble ending, were about to cease.

Prominent and successful leaders are always people who reach decisions quickly, yet it is not to be assumed that quick decisions are always advisable. There are circumstances calling for deliberation, the study of *facts* connected with the intended *decision,* etc. However, after *all* available facts have been gathered and organized, there is no excuse for delaying *decision,* and the person who practices the habit of such *delay* cannot become an effective leader until he masters this shortcoming.

Julius Caesar had long wanted to conquer the armies of another country, but he faltered because he was not sure of the loyalty *of his own* armies. Finally he decided upon a plan which would insure this loyalty. Loading his soldiers on boats he set sail for the shores of his enemy, unloaded the soldiers and implements of war, and then gave the order for all the boats to be burned. Turning to his generals he said, "Now it is win or perish! We have no choice! Pass the word to your men and let them know that it is the lives of our enemies or our own." They went into battle and won—won because all his soldiers had reached a *decision to win!*

Grant said, "We will fight it out along these lines if it takes all summer," and despite his deficiencies he stood by that *decision* and won!

When asked by one of his sailors what he would do if they saw no signs of land by the following day, Columbus replied, "If we see no land to-morrow we will sail on and on." He, too, had a *definite chief aim,* a *definite plan* for its attainment, and he had reached a *decision* not to turn back.

It is a known fact that many men cannot do their best until they are actually fighting with their backs to the wall, under the stress of the most urgent necessity. Impending danger will enable a man to develop super-human courage and strength of both body and mind far out of proportion to that normally used.

Napoleon, when surprised by the enemy, having dis-covered that there was a deep camouflaged ditch just ahead of the line of march of his armies, gave the order for his cavalry to charge. He waited until the dead bod-ies of men and horses filled the ditch, then marched his soldiers across and whipped the enemy. That required *decision;* moreover, it required *instantaneous decision.* One minute of faltering or hesitation and he would have been flanked by the enemy and captured. He did the unex-pected, the "impossible," and got away with it.

In the field of selling nearly all salesmen are met with the stereotyped alibi, "I will think it over and let you know later," which really means that "I do not wish to buy, but I lack the courage to reach a definite *decision* and frankly say so." Being a leader, and understanding the value of *initiative,* the real salesman does not take such alibis for an

There is a mistaken idea floating around that a man should be paid for that which he knows. In reality a man is paid for that which he does with what he knows, or that which he can get others to do with it.

answer. The real salesman begins, immediately, to assist the prospective purchaser in the process of "thinking it over" and in short order the job is completed and the sale has been made.

LESSON SIX

Imagination

No man ever accomplished anything, never created anything, never built any plan or developed a *definite chief aim* without the use of his *imagination!*

Everything that any man ever created or built was first visioned, in his own mind, through *imagination!*

Years before it became a reality the late John Wanamaker saw, in his own *imagination,* in practically all of its details, the gigantic business which now bears his name, and despite the fact that he was then without the capital to create such a business, he managed to get it and lived to see the business he had dreamed of in his mind become a splendid reality.

In the workshop of the *imagination* one may take old, well-known ideas or concepts, or parts of ideas, and combine them with still other old ideas or parts of ideas, and out of this combination create that which seems to be new. This process is the major principle of all invention.

One may have a *definite chief aim* and a plan for achieving it; may possess *self-confidence* in abundance; may have a highly developed *habit of saving,* and both *initiative* and *leadership* in abundance, but if the element of *imagination* is missing these other qualities will be held useless, because there will be no driving force to shape the use of these qualities. In the workshop of the *imagination* all plans are created, and without plans, no achievement is possible except by mere accident.

Witness the manner in which the *imagination* can be used as both the beginning and the end of successful plans: Clarence Saunders, who created the well-known chain of Piggly-Wiggly self-help grocery stores, conceived the idea on which the stores were based, or rather borrowed it, from the cafeteria restaurant system. While working as a grocer's helper Mr. Saunders went into a cafeteria for lunch. Standing in line, waiting for his turn at the food counters, the wheels of his *imagination* began to turn, and he reasoned, to himself, something like this:

"People seem to like to stand in line and help themselves. Moreover, I see that more people can be served this way, with fewer salespeople. Why would it not be a good idea to introduce this plan in the grocery business, so people could come in, wander around with a basket, pick up what they wanted, and pay on the way out?"

Then and there, with that bit of elementary "*imagining*," Mr. Saunders sowed the seed of an idea which later became the Piggly-Wiggly stores system and made him a multimillionaire in the bargain.

"Ideas" are the most profitable products of the human mind, and they are all created in the *imagination*. The five and ten cent store system is the result of *imagination*. The system was created by F. W. Woolworth, and it "happened" in this way: Woolworth was working as a salesman in a retail store. The owner of the store complained that he had a considerable amount of old, unsalable merchandise on hand that was in the way, and was about to throw some of it into the trash box to be consigned to the furnace, when Woolworth's *imagination* began to function.

"I have an idea," said he, "how to make this merchandise sell. Let's put it all on a table and place a big sign on the table saying that all articles will be sold at ten cents each."

The "idea" seemed feasible; it was tried, worked satisfactorily, and then began further development which resulted, finally, in the big chain of Woolworth stores which belted the entire country and made the man who used his *imagination* a multimillionaire.

Ideas are valuable in any business, and the man who makes it his business to cultivate the power of *imagination,* out of which ideas are born, will sooner or later find himself headed toward financial success with tremendous power back of him.

Thomas A. Edison invented the incandescent electric light bulb by the use of his *imagination,* when he assembled two old and well-known principles in a combination in which they had never before been associated. A brief description of just how this was accomplished will help you to vision the manner in which the *imagination* may be made to solve problems, overcome obstacles and lay the foundation for great achievements in any undertaking.

Mr. Edison discovered, as other experimenters had before him, that a light could be created by applying electrical energy to a wire, thus heating the wire to a white heat. The trouble, however, came because of the fact that no one had found a way to control the heat. The wire soon burned out when heated sufficiently to give a clear light.

After many years of experimentation Mr. Edison happened to think of the old, well-known method of burning charcoal, and saw, instantly, that this principle held the secret to the needed control of heat essential in creating a light by applying electrical power to a wire.

Charcoal is made by placing a pile of wood on the ground, setting the wood on fire, and then covering it over with dirt, thereby cutting off most of the oxygen from the fire, which enables the wood to burn slowly, but it cannot blaze and the stick cannot burn up entirely. This because there can be no combustion where there is no oxygen, and but little combustion where there is but little oxygen. With this knowledge in mind Edison went into his laboratory, placed the wire, with which he had been experimenting, inside a vacuum tube, thus cutting off *all* the oxygen, applied the electrical power, and lo! he had a perfect incandescent light bulb. The wire inside the bulb could not burn up because there was no oxygen inside to create combustion sufficient to burn it up.

Thus it happened that one of the most useful of modern inventions was created by combining two principles in a new way.

There is nothing absolutely new!

That which seems to be new is but a combination of ideas or elements of something old. This is literally true in the creation of business plans, invention, the manufacture of metals, and everything else created by man.

What is known as a "basic" patent is rarely offered for record at the Patent Office, meaning a patent that embraces really new and heretofore undiscovered principles. Most of the hundreds of thousands of patents applied for and granted every year, many of which are of a most useful nature, involve nothing more than a new arrangement or combination of old and well-known principles which have been used many times before in other ways and for other purposes.

When Mr. Saunders created his famous Piggly-Wiggly stores system, he did not even combine two ideas; he merely took an old idea that he saw in use *and gave it a new setting,* or in other words, put it to a new use, but this required *imagination.*

To cultivate the *imagination* so it will eventually suggest ideas on its own initiative, you should make it your business to keep a record of all the useful, ingenious and practical ideas you see in use in other lines of work outside of your own occupation, as well as in connection with your own work. Start with an ordinary, pocket-size notebook, and catalogue every idea, or concept, or thought that occurs to you which is capable of practical use, and then take these ideas and work them into new plans. By and by the time will come when the powers of your own *imagination* will go into the storehouse of your own subconscious mind, where all the knowledge you have ever gathered is stored, assemble this knowledge into new combinations, and hand over to you the results in the shape of *brand new ideas,* or what appear to be new ideas.

This procedure is practical because it has been followed successfully by some of the best-known leaders, inventors, and business men.

Let us here define the word *imagination* as "The workshop of the mind wherein may be assembled, in new and varying combinations, all ideas, thoughts, plans, facts, principles, and theories known to man."

A single combination of ideas, which may be merely parts of old and well-known ideas, may be worth anywhere from a few cents to a few millions of dollars. Imagination is the one faculty on which there is no set price or value. It is the most important of the faculties of the mind, for it is here that all of man's motives are given the impulse necessary to turn them into *action*.

The dreamer, who does nothing more than dream, uses imagination, but he falls short of utilizing this great faculty efficiently because he does not add to it the impulse to put his thoughts into *action*. Here is where *initiative* enters and goes to work for him, providing he is familiar with the Laws of Success and understands that ideas, of themselves, are worthless until put into action.

The dreamer who creates practical ideas must place back of these ideas three of the laws which have preceded this one, on *imagination*, namely:

1. The Law of a Definite Chief Aim
2. The Law of Self-Confidence
3. The Law of Initiative and Leadership

Without the influence of these three laws no man may put into action his thoughts and ideas, although the power to dream, imagine, and create may be highly developed.

It is your business to succeed in life! How? That is something you must answer for yourself, but, in the main, you must proceed something after this order:

1. Adopt a definite purpose and create a definite plan for its attainment.
2. Take the initiative and begin putting your plan into action.
3. Back your initiative with belief in yourself and in your ability to successfully complete your plan.

No matter who you are, what you are doing, how much your income is, how little money you have, if you have a sound mind and if you are capable of using your *imagination*, you can gradually make a place for yourself that will command for you respect and give you all the worldly goods that you need. There is no trick connected with this. The procedure is simple, as you may start with a very simple, elementary idea, plan, or purpose, and gradually develop it into something more pretentious.

Your *imagination* may not be sufficiently developed, at this time, to enable you to create some useful invention, but you can begin exercising this faculty by using it to create ways and means of improving the methods of performing your present work, whatever it may be. Your *imagination* will grow strong in proportion to the extent that you command it and direct it into use. Look about you and you will find plenty of opportunities to exercise your *imagination*. Do not wait for someone to show you what to do, but use vision and let your *imagination* suggest what to do. Do not wait for someone to pay you for using your *imagination,* because your real pay will come from the fact that every time you use it constructively, in creating new combinations of ideas, it will grow stronger, and if you keep up this practice the time will come, very soon, when your services will be sought eagerly, at any price within reason.

If a man works in a gasoline filling station, for example, it may seem to him that he has but little range of opportunity to use his *imagination*. Nothing could be further from the real facts, for as a matter of fact, any man holding such a position may give his *imagination* the very finest sort of exercise by making it his business to cultivate every motorist whom he serves in such a manner that the motorist will come back for more service. Moreover, he may go a step further and work out ways and means of adding one new customer each day, or even one a week, or one a month, and in that manner very materially and quickly add to his income. Sooner or later, through this sort of exercise of his *imagination,* backed up by *self-confidence* and *initiative,* plus a *definite chief aim,* the man who follows this practice will be sure to create some new plan that will draw customers to his filling station from far and near, and he will then be on the great Highway to Success.

A complete analysis of occupations shows that the most profitable occupation on earth, taken as a whole, is that of salesmanship. The man whose fertile mind and *imagination* create a new and useful invention may not have sufficient ability to market his invention, and may therefore have to dispose of it for a mere pittance, as is, in fact, so often the case; but the man who has the ability to market that invention may (and generally does) make a fortune out of it.

Any man who can create plans and ideas that will cause the number of patrons of any business to constantly increase, and who is able to send all the patrons away satisfied, is well on the way toward *success*, regardless of the commodity, service, or wares he may be selling.

It is not the purpose of this brief outline of the Law of Success philosophy to show the student what to do and how to do it, but the general rules of procedure which apply in all successful undertakings have been here enumerated so anyone may understand them. These rules are simple and easily adopted by anyone.

LESSON SEVEN

Enthusiasm

It seems more than a mere coincidence that the most successful people, in all walks of life—and particularly is this true in selling—are of the enthusiastic type.

Enthusiasm is a driving force which not only gives greater power to the man who has it, but it is contagious and affects all whom it reaches. Enthusiasm over the work in which one is engaged takes the drudgery out of that work. It has been observed that laborers, engaged in the toilsome job of ditch digging, can take the drabness out of their f work by singing as they work.

When the "Yanks" went into action, during the World War, they went in singing and full of enthusiasm. This was too much for the war-worn soldiers who had been in the field long enough to wear off their enthusiasm, and they made poor match indeed for the "Yanks."

The Filene Department Store, in Boston, is opened with music furnished by the store band every morning during the summer months. The sales people dance to the music, catch the rhythm of the tunes, and when the doors are finally opened for business the patrons of the store meet a jolly crowd of enthusiastic, cheerful, smiling sales people, many of whom are still softly humming the tune to which they had been dancing but a few minutes before. This spirit of enthusiasm remains with the sales people throughout the day. It lightens their work and creates an "atmosphere" in the store which is pleasing to the customers.

During the World War, it was discovered that, by introducing music, with the aid of bands and orchestras, etc., into the plants where war materials were being made, production was stimulated, in some instances as much as fifty per cent above normal production without the music. Moreover, it was discovered that the workers not only turned out much more work during the day, but they came to the end of the day without fatigue, many of them whistling or singing on their way home. Enthusiasm gives greater power to one's efforts, no matter what sort of work one may be engaged in.

The starting point of enthusiasm is "motive," or well-defined desire. Enthusiasm is simply a high rate of vibration of the mind. Elsewhere in this book may be found a complete list of the mind stimulants which will super-induce the state of mind known as enthusiasm. The urge of sexual desire is the greatest known mind stimulant. People who do not feel a strong desire for sexual contact are seldom, if ever, capable of becoming highly enthusiastic over anything. Transmutation of the great driving force of sex desire is the basis of practically all the works of genius. (By "transmutation" is meant the switching of thought from sexual contact to any other form of physical action.)

The importance of enthusiasm, as one of the seventeen essentials of the Law of Success, is explained in the chapter on the Master Mind. The strange phenomenon felt by those who co-ordinate their efforts, in a spirit of harmony, for the purpose of availing themselves of the Master Mind principle, is merely a high rate of vibration of their minds known as enthusiasm.

It is a well-known fact that men succeed most readily when engaged in an occupation which they like best, and this for the reason that they readily become enthusiastic over that which they like best. Enthusiasm is also the basis of creative imagination. When the mind is vibrating at a high rate, it is receptive to similar high rates of vibration, from outside sources, thus providing a favorable condition for creative imagination. It will be observed that enthusiasm plays an important part in four of the other principles constituting the Law of Success philosophy, namely, the Master Mind, Imagination, Accurate Thought, and Pleasing Personality.

Enthusiasm, to be of value, must be controlled and directed to definite ends. Uncontrolled enthusiasm may be, and generally is, destructive. The acts of so-called "bad boys" are nothing more nor less than uncontrolled enthusiasm. The wasted energy of uncontrolled enthusiasm expressed through promiscuous sexual contact, and sex desire not expressed through contact, by the majority of young men, is sufficient to lift them to high achievement if this urge were harnessed and transformed into some other form of physical action.

The next chapter, on Self-Control, appropriately follows the subject of Enthusiasm, as much self-control is necessary in the mastery of enthusiasm.

LESSON EIGHT

Self-Control

Lack of Self-Control has brought grief to more people than any other one shortcoming known to the human race. This evil shows itself, at one time or another, in every person's life.

Every successful person must have some sort of a balance wheel for his or her emotions. When a person "loses his temper," something takes place in his brain which should be better understood. When a person becomes extremely angry, the suprarenal glands begin to empty their contents into the blood, and if this is kept up for any great length of time the amount will be sufficient to do serious damage to the entire system, sometimes resulting in death.

Suprarenal is Nature's "repair kit" with which she causes the blood to coagulate and stop the flow, in the event of injury. Anger immediately excites the suprarenal glands and their contents begin to pour into the blood. This accounts for one turning white and red in the face, alternately, as the flow of blood throughout the body is temporarily checked. No doubt Nature created this system for man's protection during the savage stage of his development, when anger usually preceded a terrific fight with some other savage, which might mean opening of the veins and loss of blood.

Scientists have found, by experiment, that a dog will, when tormented until it becomes angry, throw off enough poison with each exhalation of breath to kill a guinea pig. An angry man will do the same.

But there are other reasons why one should develop Self-Control. For example, the man who lacks Self-Control may be easily mastered by one who has such control, and tricked into saying or doing that which may later be embarrassing to him.

Success in life is very largely a matter of harmonious negotiation with other people, and this requires Self-Control in abundance.

The author of the Law of Success philosophy once observed a long line of angry women in front of the "Complaint Desk" of a large Chicago department store. Watching at a distance, it was seen that the young woman, who was hearing the complaints, kept sweetly cool and smiled all the while, notwithstanding the fact that some of the women were very abusive. One by one this young woman directed the women to the right depart-

> If you wish to sell me something be sure to create for me a plan through which I can harness that which you wish to sell me so it will help pull my load and I will be more eager to buy than you are to sell.

ment, and she did it with such poise that it caused the author to walk up closer where he could see just what was happening. Standing just back of the young woman at the Complaint Desk was another young woman who was also listening to the conversations, and making notes and passing them over the shoulder of the young woman who was actually handling the Desk.

These notes contained the gist of each complaint, minus the vitriol and abuse of the person making the complaint. *The woman at the desk was stone deaf!* She was getting all the facts that she needed through her assistant, at her back.

The manager of the store said that this was the only system he had found that enabled him to handle the Complaint Desk properly, as human nerves were not strong enough to listen all day long, day in and day out, to abusive language without causing the person doing the listening to become angry, lose Self-Control, and "strike back."

An angry man is suffering with a degree of temporary insanity, and therefore he is hardly capable of diplomatic negotiation with others. For this reason the angry man, or the one who has no Self-Control, is an easy victim of the man who has such control. No man may become powerful without first gaining control of himself.

Self-Control is also a balance wheel for the person who is too optimistic and whose *enthusiasm* needs checking, for it is possible to become entirely too enthusiastic; so much so that one becomes a bore to all those near him.

The Habit of Doing More than Paid For

This law is a stumblingblock on which many a promising career has been shattered. There is a general attitude among people to perform just as little service as they can get by with, but if you will study these people carefully, you will observe that while they may be actually "getting by" temporarily, they are not, however, getting anything else.

There are two major reasons why all successful people must practice this Law, as follows:

1. Just as an arm or a limb of the body grows strong in exact proportion to its use, so does the mind grow strong through use. By rendering the greatest possible amount of service the faculties through which the

service is rendered are put into use and, eventually, become strong and accurate,

2. By rendering more service than that for which you are paid, you will be turning the spotlight of *favorable* attention upon yourself, and it will not be long before you will be sought with fancy offers for your services, and there will be a continuous market for those services,

"Do the thing and you shall have the power," was the admonition of Emerson, the great modern philosopher.

That is literally true! Practice makes perfect. The better you do your work, the more adept you become at doing it, and this, in time, will lead to such perfection that you will have but few, if any, equals in your field of endeavor.

By rendering more service and better service than that for which you are paid, you thereby take advantage of the Law of Increasing Returns through the operation of which you will eventually be paid, in one way or another, for far more service than you actually perform.

This is no mere finely spun theory. It actually works out in the most practical tests. You must not imagine, however, that the Law always works instantaneously. You may render more service and better service than you are supposed to render for a few days, then discontinue the practice and go back to the old, usual habit of doing as little as can be safely trusted to get you by, and the results will in no way benefit you. But adopt the habit as a part of your life's philosophy, and let it become known by all who know you that you render such service out of choice, not as a matter of accident, but by *deliberate intent,* and soon you will see keen competition for your service.

You will not find very many people rendering such service, which is all the better for you, because you will stand out in bold contrast with practically all others who are engaged in work similar to yours. Contrast is a powerful law, and you may, in this manner, profit by contrast.

Some people set up the weak argument that it does not pay to render more service and better service than one is paid to render because it is not appreciated, and that they work for people who are selfish and will not recognize such service.

Splendid! The more selfish an employer is the more apt he will be inclined to wish to hold the services of a person who makes it his business to render such unusual service, that is greater in quantity and better in quality than most people render. This very selfishness will "force" such an employer to recognize such services. However, if he should happen to be the proverbial exception who has not sufficient vision to analyze those who work for him, then it is only a matter of time until all who render such service will attract the attention of other employers who will gladly reward that sort of service.

Careful study of the lives of successful men has shown that faithfully practicing this one Law alone has brought the usual emoluments in which success is measured in plentiful quantities. If the author of this philosophy had to choose one of the Seventeen Laws of Success as being the most important, and had to discard all the others except the one chosen, he would, without a moment's hesitation, choose this Law of *Rendering More Service and Better Service than Paid for.*

A Pleasing Personality

A Pleasing Personality, naturally, is a personality that docs not antagonize. Personality cannot be defined in one word, not with half a dozen words, for it represents the sum total of all one's characteristics, good and bad.

Your Personality is totally unlike any other personality. It is the sum total of qualities, emotions, characteristics, appearances, etc., which distinguish you from all other people on earth.

Your clothes form an important part of your personality; the way you wear them, the harmony of colors you select, the quality and many other details all go to indicate much that belongs distinctly as a part of your personality. The psychologists claim that they can accurately analyze any person, in many important respects, by turning that person loose in a clothing store where there is a great variety of clothing, with instructions to select whatever may be wanted and dress in the clothes selected.

Your facial expression, as shown by the lines of your face, or the lack of lines, forms an important part of your personality. Your voice, its pitch, tone, volume, and the language you use form important parts of your personality, because they mark you instantly, once you have spoken, as a person of refinement or the opposite.

The manner in which you shake hands constitutes an important port of your Personality. If, when shaking hands, you merely hold out a cold "hunk" of flesh and bones that is limp and lifeless, you are displaying a sign of a Personality that is not mixed with *enthusiasm* or *initiative*.

A Pleasing Personality usually may be found in the person who speaks gently and kindly, selecting refined words that do not offend, in a modest tone of voice; who selects clothing of appropriate style and colors which harmonize; who is unselfish and not only willing, but desirous of serving others; who is a friend of all humanity, the rich and the poor alike, regardless of politics, religion, or occupation; who refrains from speaking unkindly of others, either with or without cause; who manages to converse without being drawn into vulgar conversations or useless arguments on such debatable subjects as religion and politics; who sees both the good and the bad in people, but makes due allowance for the latter; who seeks neither to reform nor to reprimand others; who smiles frequently and deeply; who loves music and little children; who sympathizes with all who are in trouble and forgives acts of unkindness; who willingly grants others the right to do as they please as long as no one's rights are interfered with; who earnestly strives to be constructive in every thought and deed indulged in; who encourages others and spurs them on to greater and better achievement in their chosen line of work.

A Pleasing Personality is something that can be acquired by anyone who has the determination to learn how to negotiate his or her way through life without friction, with the object of getting along peacefully and quietly with others.

One of the best-known and most successful men in America once said that he would prefer a Pleasing Personality, as it is defined in this course, to the college degree that was awarded him, more than fifty years ago, by Harvard University. It was his opinion that a man could accomplish more with a Pleasing Personality than he could with a college degree, minus the personality.

The development of a Pleasing Personality calls for exercise of Self-Control, because there will be many incidents and many people to try your patience and destroy your good resolutions to become pleasing. The reward is worthy of the effort, however, because one who possesses a Pleasing Personality stands out so boldly in contrast with the majority of people around him, that his pleasing qualities become all the more pronounced.

When Abraham Lincoln was a young man, he heard that a great lawyer, who was known to be an impressive orator, was to defend a client charged with murder, some forty miles from Lincoln's home. He walked the entire distance to hear this man, who was one of the spellbinders of the South. After he had heard the man's speech, and the orator was on his way out of the court room, Lincoln stepped into the aisle, held out his rough hand, and said, "I walked forty miles to hear you, and if I were to do it over, I would walk a hundred."

The lawyer looked young Lincoln over, turned up his nose, and, in a supercilious manner, walked out without speaking to Lincoln.

Years later these two met once again, this time in the White House, where this selfsame lawyer had come to petition the "President of the United States" in behalf of a man who had been condemned to death.

Lincoln listened patiently to all the lawyer had to say, and, when he had finished speaking, said, "I see you have lost none of your eloquence since I first heard you defend a murderer years ago, but you have changed considerably in other ways, because you now seem to be a polite gentleman of refinement, which was not the impression I got of you at our first meeting. I did you an injustice, perhaps, for which I now ask your pardon. Meanwhile, I shall sign a pardon for your client and we will call accounts square."

The lawyer's face turned white and red as he stammered a brief apology!

By his lack of a Pleasing Personality, at his first meeting with Lincoln, he was guilty of conduct which would have been costly to him, had the incident happened with one less charitable than the great Lincoln.

It has been said, and perhaps correctly, that "courtesy" represents the most valuable characteristic known to the human race. Courtesy costs nothing, yet it returns dividends that are stupendous if it is practiced as a matter of habit, in a spirit of sincerity.

A young friend of the author of this philosophy was employed as a service man in one of the gasoline filling stations belonging to a large corporation. One day a big car drove up to his station, and the man on the inside stepped out while the chauffeur purchased gas. While the gas was being delivered, this man entered into conversation with my young friend—or, perhaps I should more truthfully say—my young "acquaintance."

"Do you like your job?" the man inquired.

"Like it, hell!" replied the young bravo. "I like it just as much as a dog loves a tomcat."

"Well," said the stranger, "if you do not like your job, why do you work here?"

"Because I am just waiting for something better to turn up," was the quick rejoinder.

"How long do you think you will have to wait?" the man inquired.

"I dunno how long, but I hope I soon get out of here, because there is no opportunity here for a bright fellow like myself. Why, I'm a high school graduate and I can hold a better position if I had it."

"Yes?" said the stranger. "*If!* Now if I offered you a better position than the one you now have, would you be any better off than you are now?"

"I can't say," replied the service station man.

"Well," replied the stranger, "may I not offer the suggestion that better positions usually come to those who are prepared to fill them, but I do not believe you are ready for a better position; at least not while you are in your present frame of mind. Perhaps there is a big opportunity for you right where you stand. Let me recommend that you buy a copy of Russell Conwell's book, *Acres of Diamonds*, as it may give you an idea that will be useful to you all through life."

The stranger got into his automobile and drove away. He was the president of the company that owned the filling station. The young man was talking to his employer, without knowing it, but every word he uttered spoiled his chances of attracting *favorable* attention.

Later this same filling station was placed in charge of another young man, and it is one of the most profitable service stations operated by the company which owns it. The station is the same as it was before it was turned over to new management. The supplies sold are exactly the same. The prices charged are the same, *but* the Personality of the man who meets and impresses favorably or unfavorably those who drive up to this station for service is *not the same*.

Practically all success in life hinges, in the final analysis, on *personality*.

A nasty disposition can spoil the chances of the best educated man, and such dispositions do spoil not a few such men.

Good Showmanship a Part of Personality

Life may be properly called a great drama in which good showmanship is of the utmost importance. Successful people, in all callings, are generally good showmen; meaning, by this, that they practice the habit of catering or playing to the crowd. Let us compare some well-known men on the subject of their ability as showmen. The following men have enjoyed outstanding success in their respective callings, because of good showmanship:

Henry L. Doherty	Theodore Roosevelt
Bernarr Macfadden	Henry Ford

Thomas A. Edison

Billy Sunday

E. M. Statler

John H. Patterson

Wm. Randolph Hearst

Wm. C. Durant

Geo. Bernard Shaw

Arthur Brisbane

Following is a list of some well-known men, each a man of great ability, but falling short by comparison with the foregoing list, on the score of good showmanship:

Woodrow Wilson

Calvin Coolidge

Herbert Hoover

Abraham Lincoln

Dr. Elmer Gates

A good showman is one who understands how to cater to the masses. Success is not a matter of chance or luck. It is the result of careful planning and careful staging and able acting of parts by the players in the game.

What is to be done about his defect by the man who is not blessed with a personality which lends itself to able showmanship? Is such a person to be doomed to failure all his life because of Nature's oversight in not blessing him with such a personality?

Not at all! Here is where the principle of the Master Mind comes to the rescue. Those who do not have pleasing personalities may surround themselves with men and women who supply this defect. The late J. P. Morgan had a rather pugnacious attitude toward people which prevented him from being a good showman. However, he associated with himself others who supplied all that he lacked in this respect.

Henry Ford was not blessed, by Nature, with native ability as a good showman, and his personality is not one hundred per cent perfect by a long way, but, knowing how to make use of the Master Mind principle, he bridged this defect by surrounding himself with men who do have such ability.

What are the most essential characteristics of good showmanship?

First, the ability to appeal to the imagination of the public, and to keep people interested and curious concerning one's activities. Second, a keen sense of appreciation of the value of psychological appeal through advertising. Third, sufficient alertness of mind to enable one to capture and make use of the prejudices, likes, and dislikes of the public, at the psychological moment.

Summary of Factors Which Constitute a Pleasing Personality

Following is a condensed description of the major factors which serve as the basis of a Pleasing Personality:

1. Manner of shaking hands
2. Clothing and posture of the body
3. Voice, its tone, volume, and quality
4. Tactfulness

5. Sincerity of purpose

6. Choice of words, and their appropriateness

7. Poise

8. Unselfishness

9. Facial expression

10. Dominating thoughts (Which register in the minds of other people)

11. Enthusiasm

12. Honesty (Intellectual, moral, and economic)

13. *Magnetism* (High rate of vibration due to well-defined sexual urge)

If you wish to try an interesting and perhaps a beneficial experiment, analyze yourself and give yourself a grading on each of these thirteen factors of a Pleasing Personality. An accurate check-up on these thirteen points might easily bring to one's notice facts which would enable one to eliminate faults which make success impossible.

It will also be an interesting experiment if you form the habit of analyzing those whom you know intimately, measuring them by the thirteen points here described. Such a habit will, in time, help you to find in other people the causes of both success and failure.

Accurate Thinking

The art of Accurate Thinking is not difficult to acquire, although certain definite rules must be followed. To think accurately one must follow at least two basic principles, as follows:

1. Accurate Thinking calls for the separation of *facts* from mere *information*.

2. *Facts*, when ascertained, must be separated into two classes; one is known as *important* and the other as *unimportant*, or irrelevant.

The question naturally arises, "What is an *important fact?*" and the answer is, "An *important fact* is any fact essential for the attainment of one's *definite chief aim* or purpose, or which may be useful or necessary in connection with one's daily occupation. All other facts, while they may be useful and interesting, are comparatively unimportant as far as the individual is concerned."

No man has the right to have an opinion on any subject, unless he has arrived at that opinion by a process of reasoning that is based upon all the available *facts* connected with the subject of the opinion. Despite this fact, however, nearly everyone has opinions on nearly every subject, whether they are familiar with those subjects or have any *facts* connected with them or not.

Snap judgments and opinions that are not opinions at all, but mere wild conjectures or guesses, are valueless; "there's not an *idea* in a carload" of them. Any man may become an Accurate Thinker by making it his business to insist upon getting the Facts, all that are available with reasonable effort, before reaching decisions or creating opinions on any subject.

When you hear a man begin a discourse with such generalities as "I hear that so and so is the case," or, "I see by the papers that so and so did so and so," you may put that man down as one who is *not* an Accurate Thinker, and his opinions, guesses, statements, and conjectures should be accepted, if at all, with a good big handful of the proverbial salt of caution.

Be careful, also, that *you* do not indulge in wild, speculative language that is not based upon *known facts*.

It often requires considerable effort to *know facts* on any subject, which is perhaps the main reason why so few people take the time or go to the trouble to gather *facts* as the basis of their opinions.

You are presumably following this philosophy for the purpose of learning how you may become more successful, and if that is true then *you* must break away from the common practices of the masses who do not think and take the time to gather *facts* as the basis of your thoughts. That this requires effort is freely admitted, but it must be kept in mind that *success* is not something that one may come along and pluck from a tree, where it has grown of its own accord. Success is something that represents perseverance, self-sacrifice, determination, and strong character.

Everything has its price, and nothing may be obtained without paying this price; or, if something of value is obtained, it cannot be retained for long. The price of Accurate Thought is the effort required to gather and organize the *facts* on which to base the *thought*.

"How many automobiles pass this filling station each day," the manager of a chain of filling stations asked a new service man. "And on what days is traffic the heaviest?"

"I am of the opinion . . ." the young man began.

"Never mind your *opinion*," the manager interrupted. "What I asked you calls for an answer based upon *facts*. Opinions are worth nothing when the actual *facts* are obtainable."

With the aid of a pocket adder this young man began to count the automobiles that passed his station each day. He went a step further and recorded the number that actually stopped and purchased supplies, giving the figures day by day for two weeks, including Sundays.

> Time is a master worker which heals the wounds of failure and disappointment and equalizes the inequalities and rights the wrongs of the world. Nothing is IMPOSSIBLE with TIME.

Nor was this all! He estimated the number of automobiles that should have stopped at his station for supplies, day by day, for two weeks. Going still further, he created a plan that cost only a one-cent postal card per motorist, that actually increased the number of automobiles that stopped at his station for service the following two weeks. This was not a part of his required duties, but the question asked him by his manager had put him to *thinking*, and he made up his mind to profit by the incident.

The young man in question is now a half owner in a chain of filling stations of his own, and a moderately wealthy man, thanks to his ability to become an Accurate Thinker.

LESSON TWELVE

Concentration

The jack-of-all-trades seldom accomplishes much at any trade. Life is so complex, and there are so many ways of dissipating energy unprofitably, that the habit of *concentrated effort* must be formed and adhered to by all who succeed.

Power is based upon organized effort or energy. Energy cannot be organized without the habit of *concentration* of all the faculties on one thing at a time. An ordinary reading glass may be used GQ so focus the rays of the sun that they will burn a hole in a board in a few minutes. Those same rays will not even heat the board until they are *concentrated* on one spot.

The human mind is something like the reading glass, because it is the medium through which all the faculties of the brain may be brought together and made to function, in co-ordinated formation, just as the rays of the sun may be focused on one spot with the aid of a reading glass.

It is worthy of serious consideration to remember that all the outstanding men of success, in all walks of life, concentrated the major portion of their thoughts and efforts upon some one *definite purpose*, objective, or *chief aim*.

Witness the impressive list of men whose success is due to their having acquired and practiced the habit of *concentration:*

Woolworth concentrated upon the single idea of five and ten cent stores and the result made of him a multi-millionaire.

Henry Ford concentrated all his energies upon the single aim of creating a cheap but practical automobile, and that idea made of him the most powerful and the richest man who ever lived on this earth.

Marshall Field concentrated his efforts upon building "The World's Greatest Store" and was rewarded by tens of millions of dollars. The great Field Store, in Chicago, is a living monument to the soundness of the practice of *concentration.*

Van Heusen concentrated years of efforts on the production of a soft collar, and the idea made him wealthy in a comparatively short time.

Wrigley concentrated his efforts upon the production and sale of a humble five-cent package of chewing gum and was rewarded by millions of dollars for his perseverance.

Edison concentrated his mind upon the production of the talking machine, the electric light, the moving picture, and scores of other useful inventions, and they all became realities and made of Edison a wealthy man.

Edwin C. Barnes concentrated his mind upon becoming a business associate of Thomas A. Edison, and not only accomplished the desired end, but made several million dollars for himself and has now retired from active business, while still a comparatively young man.

Bessemer concentrated his thoughts upon a better way to produce steel and the now-famous Bessemer process is evidence that his efforts were not without reward.

George Eastman concentrated his energy upon producing the best kodak, and this one idea has made of him a multimillionaire.

Andrew Carnegie visioned a great steel industry, concentrated his mind upon that purpose, and made tens of millions of dollars.

James J. Hill, while still working as a telegrapher at forty dollars a month, concentrated upon a great transcontinental railway system and kept on thinking about it *(and acting on his thought as well)* until it became a splendid reality and made him one of the wealthy men of his time.

Cyrus H. K. Curtis concentrated his efforts upon one idea of producing the best and most popular magazine on earth, and the splendid *Saturday Evening Post* was but one of the results. He not only created a great magazine, but his concentration of thought brought him millions as well.

Orville Wright concentrated upon the one purpose of mastering the air with a heavier-than-air machine, and accomplished it within the memory of all now living.

Edward W. Bok could not speak English when he first came to this country, but very soon determined to become a great magazine editor, and his concentrated efforts made the *Ladies' Home Journal* a great periodical, and himself a wealthy man.

Marconi concentrated his mind upon the one thought of sending wireless messages, and now the sound of the human voice may be sent around the earth, without trouble.

Truly, whatever man can *imagine,* man can create, providing he *concentrates* his mind upon it with determination not to stop short of victory

Dr. Gunsaulus was a young preacher who had an idea that required a million dollars for its development. He concentrated his mind upon the task and wrote one sermon which got him the million dollars the first time he delivered it.

Great and powerful is the human mind when functioning through the aid of *concentrated thought.*

Woodrow Wilson determined to become President of the United States twenty-five years before he actually occupied the President's chair in the White House, but he kept his mind concentrated upon this one purpose and eventually achieved it.

Henry L. Doherty concentrated on the organization and management of public utilities and became one of the most extensive and wealthy operators in this field.

Ingersoll concentrated on the production of a good, practical watch that could be sold for one dollar and his idea, plus his concentrated efforts, made of him a multi-millionaire.

E. M. Stader concentrated on the building of hotels that render home-like service, without the annoyance of tips, and has made himself the leading hotel man of the world, to say nothing of many millions of dollars in wealth.

Martin W Littleton heard a speech, when he was a small boy, which caused him to concentrate his mind upon the one idea of becoming the best lawyer in the United States, and it is said that he now accepts no fee under $25,000, yet he is kept busy all the time.

Rockefeller concentrated his efforts upon the refining and distribution of oil, and his efforts brought him tens of millions of dollars.

Russell Conwell concentrated a lifetime of effort on the delivery of his famous lecture, *Acres of Diamonds,* and that one lecture brought in more than six million dollars, and rendered the world a service the extent of which can never be estimated in mere money.

Lincoln concentrated his mind upon freedom for mankind, and saw his task through to an unfortunate end.

Gillette concentrated upon producing a safety razor, and the idea made him a multimillionaire.

William Randolph Hearst concentrated on newspapers, and has made millions out of his idea.

Helen Keller was born deaf, dumb, and blind, but through concentration she has learned to "hear" and to speak.

John H. Patterson concentrated upon cash registers, and the world paid him tribute in terms of millions of dollars for his idea.

So the story might go on and on in one continuous chain, as evidence that *concentrated* effort is profitable.

Find out what you wish to do—adopt a *definite chief aim*—then concentrate all your energies back of this purpose until it has reached a happy climax.

Observe, in analyzing the next Law, on *co-operation*, the close connection between the principles outlined and those associated with the Law of *Concentration*.

Wherever a group of people ally themselves in an organized, cooperative spirit for the carrying out of some definite purpose, it will be observed that they are employing the Law of *Concentration*, and unless they do so their alliance will be without real power.

Raindrops, as they fall through the air, each one for itself, helter-skelter, represent a very great form of energy, but this energy cannot be called real power until those raindrops are collected, in a river or dam, and made to pour their energy over a wheel in organized fashion; or, until they are confined in a boiler and converted into steam.

Everywhere, regardless of the form in which it is found, *power* is developed through *concentrated* energy. Whatever you are doing as your daily occupation, do it with all of your attention, all your heart and soul focused on that one definite thing.

Co-operation

This is distinctly an age of *co-operation* in which we are living. The outstanding achievements in business, industry, finance, transportation, and politics are all based upon the principle of Cooperative effort.

You can hardly read a daily paper one week in succession without seeing notice of some consolidation or merger of business or industrial interests. These mergers and friendly alliances of business are based upon *co-operation*, because co-operation brings together in a spirit of harmony of purpose all the energies, whether human or mechanical, so that they function as one, without friction.

Marshal Foch, technically at least, won the final decision in the late World War. The turning point came, as all will remember, when all the Allied Armies were placed under the direction of Foch, thus insuring perfectly co-ordinated effort, and *co-operation* such as would not have been possible under many leaders, each exerting an equal or similar amount of authority over the various allied armies.

To succeed in a big way, in any undertaking, means that one must have the friendly co-operation of others. The winning football team is the one which is best coached in the art of *co-operation*. The spirit of perfect teamwork must prevail in business, or the business will not get very far.

You will observe that some of the preceding Laws of this course must be practiced as a matter of habit before one can get perfect cooperation from others. For example, other people will not co-operate with you unless you have mastered and apply the Law of a *Pleasing Personality:* You will also notice that *Enthusiasm* and *Self-Control* and *The Habit of Doing More than Paid For* must be practiced before you can hope to gain full co-operation from others.

These Laws overlap one another, and all of them must be merged into the Law of *Co-operation*, which means that one, to gain co-operation from others, must form the habit of practicing the Laws named.

No man is willing to co-operate with a person who has an offensive Personality. No man is willing to co-operate with one who is not Enthusiastic, or who lacks Self-Control. *Power* comes from organized, *co-operative* effort!

A dozen well trained soldiers, working with perfectly co-ordinated effort, can master a mob of a thousand people who lack leadership and organization.

Education, in all of its forms, is nothing but *organized knowledge,* or, as it might be stated—co-operative facts!

Andrew Carnegie had but little schooling, yet he was a well educated man because he formed the habit of organizing his knowledge and shaping it into a *definite chief aim.* He also made use of the Law of Co-operation, as a result of which he made himself a multimillionaire; moreover, he made millionaires of scores of other men who were allied with him in his application of the Law of *Co-operation* which he so well understood.

It was Andrew Carnegie who gave the author of the Law of Success philosophy the idea upon which the entire philosophy was founded. The event is worth describing, as it involves a newly discovered Law which is the real basis of all effective *co-operation.*

The author went to interview Carnegie for the purpose of writing a story about his industrial career. The first question asked was:

"Mr. Carnegie, to what do you attribute your great success?"

"You have asked me a big question," said Carnegie, "and before I answer I would like for you to define the word 'success.' Just what do you call success?"

Before the author had time to reply, Carnegie antici-pated the reply by saying:

"By success I think you mean my money, do you not?"

The author said, "Yes, that seems to be the term that stands for success."

"Oh, well," replied Carnegie, "if you merely wish to know how I got my money—if that is what *you* call *success*—I can easily answer your question.

"To begin with, let me tell you that we have, here in this steel business, a *Master Mind*. This Master Mind is not the mind of any one person, but it is the sum total of ability, knowledge, and experience of nearly a score of men whose minds have been perfectly co-ordinated so they function as one, in a spirit of harmonious *co-operation*. These men are the ones who manage the various departments of this business. Some of them have been associated with me for many years, while others have not been here so long.

"You may be surprised to know," Carnegie continued, "that I have had to fit and try, and then fit and fey over and over again while finding men whose personalities were such that they could subordinate their own interests for the benefit of the business. One of the most import-ant places on our staff has been filled by more than a dozen men before one was finally found who could do the work required in that position and at the same time *co-operate* in a spirit of harmony, with the other members of our staff. *My one big problem has been, and always will continue to be,* the difficulty in securing the services of men who will *co-operate,* because without co-operation the Master Mind of which I speak could not exist."

In these words, or their equivalent, as I am quoting from memory, the greatest of all the steel magnates the industry has ever known laid bare the real secret of his stupendous achievements. His statement led this author to a line of research covering a period of over twenty years, which resulted in the discovery that this same principle of which Carnegie spoke is also the secret of the success of most of the other successful men of this type who are at the heads of our great industries, financial institutions, railroads, banks, department stores, etc.

It is a fact, although the scientific world may not have so endorsed it, that wherever two or more minds are allied, or associated in any undertaking, in a spirit of *perfect harmony and co-operative effort* there arises, out of this alliance, an unseen power that gives greater energy to the efforts of those associated in the alliance.

You may test this out, in your own way, by watching the reaction of your own mind when you are in the presence of those with whom you are friendly as compared with what happens when you are in the presence of those whom you do not like. Friendly association inspires one with a mysterious energy not otherwise experienced, and this great truth is the very foundation stone of the Law of *Co-operation.*

An army that is forced to fight because the soldiers are afraid they will be shot down by their own leaders may be a very effective army, but such an army never has been a match for the army that goes into action of its own accord, with every man determined to win because he believes his side ought to win.

At the beginning of the World War the Germans were sweeping everything before them. The German soldiers, at that time, went into action singing. They had been thoroughly "sold" on the idea of "kultur." Their leaders had made them think they were bound to win because they ought to win.

However, as the war went along these same soldiers became "wised up" a bit, to use a slang term. It began to dawn upon their minds that the killing off of millions of men was a serious business. Next, the thought began to creep in that, after all, perhaps their kaiser was not the ordained agent of God, and that they might be fighting an unjust war.

From this point on the tide began to turn. They no longer went into battle singing. They no longer "felt proud to die for kultur," and the end of them was then but a short distance away.

So it is in every walk of life, in every human endeavor. The man who can subordinate his own personality, subdue his own self-interests and co-ordinate all his efforts, physical and mental, with those of other men, back of a common cause, believing that what he is doing is right and should be successful, has already gone nearly the entire distance toward success.

———————

A few years ago the president of a well-known real estate company addressed the following letter to the author:

> DEAR MR. HILL:
> Our firm will give you a check for $10,000 if you will show us how to get the confidence of the public as effectively as you do in connection with the work in which you are engaged.   Very cordially,

To this letter the following reply was sent:

> DEAR MR. J—:
> May I not thank you for the compliment, and while I could use your check for $10,000, I am perfectly willing to give you, gratis, what information I have on the subject. If I have unusual ability to gain co-operation from other people, it is because of the following reasons:
>   1. I render more service than I ask people to pay for.
>   2. I engage in no transaction, intentionally, which does not benefit all whom it affects.
>   3. I make no statements which I do not believe to be true.

4. I have a sincere desire in my heart to be of useful service to the greatest possible number of people.

5. I like people better than I like money.

6. I am doing my best to *live* as well as to *teach* my own philosophy of success.

7. I accept no favors, from anyone, without giving favors in return.

8. I ask nothing of any person without having a right to that for which I ask.

9. I enter into no arguments with people over trivial matters.

10. I spread the sunshine of optimism and good cheer wherever and whenever I can.

11. I never flatter people for the purpose of gaining their confidence.

12. I sell counsel and advice to other people, at a modest price, but *never offer free advice.*

13. While teaching others how to achieve success, I have demonstrated that I can make my philosophy work for myself, as well, thus "practicing that which I preach."

14. I am so thoroughly sold on the work in which I am engaged that my enthusiasm over it becomes "contagious" and others are influenced by it.

If there are any other elements entering into what you believe to be my ability to get the confidence of others, I do not know what they are. Incidentally, your letter raised an interesting question, and caused me to analyze myself as I had never done before. For this reason I refuse to accept your check, on the ground that you have caused me to do something which may be worth many times ten thousand dollars.

Very cordially,

Napoleon Hill.

In these fourteen points may be found the elements which form the basis of all confidence-building relationships. Co-operative effort brings power to those who can gain and permanently hold the confidence of great numbers of people. This author knows of no method of inducing others to co-operate, except that which is based upon the fourteen points here described.

> Adversity is to the human being what the kiln is to the brick—it tempers the man so he can carry responsibilities and overcome obstacles without crumbling before them.

LESSON FOURTEEN

Profiting by Failure

A wealthy philosopher, by the name of Croesus, was the official counselor to his majesty, King Cyrus. He said some very wise things, in his capacity as court philosopher, among them this:

"I am reminded, O king, and take this lesson to heart, that there is a wheel on which the affairs of men revolve, and its mechanism is such that it prevents *any* man from being *always* fortunate."

It is true; there is a sort of unseen Fate, or wheel, turning in the lives of all of us, and sometimes it brings us good fortune and sometimes ill fortune, despite anything that we as individual human beings, can do. However, this wheel obeys the law of averages, thereby insuring us against continuous ill fortune. If ill fortune comes to-day, there is hope in the thought that its opposite will come in the next turn of the wheel, or the one following the next, etc.

Failure is one of the most beneficial parts of a human being's experience, for the reason that there are many needed lessons that must be learned before one commences to succeed which could be learned by no teacher other than *failure*.

Failure is always a blessing in disguise, providing it teaches us some useful lesson that we could not or would not have learned without it!

However, millions of people make the mistake of accepting *failure* as final, whereas it is, like most other events in life, but transitory, and for this reason should not be accepted as final.

Successful people must learn to distinguish between *failure* and *temporary defeat*. Every person experiences, at one time or another, some form of temporary defeat, and out of such experiences come some of the greatest and most beneficial lessons.

In truth, most of us are so constituted that if we never experienced temporary defeat (or, what some ignorantly call *failure*), we would soon become so egotistical and independent that we would imagine ourselves more important than Deity. There are a few such people in this world, and it is said of them that they refer to Deity, if at all, as "*Me* and God," with heavy emphasis on the "*Me*."

Headaches are beneficial, despite the fact that they are very disagreeable, for the reason that they represent Nature's language in which she calls loudly for intelligent use of the human body; particularly of the stomach and tributary organs through which most of us create the majority of physical human ills.

It is the same regarding Temporary Defeat or Failure—these are Nature's symbols through which she signals us that we have been headed in the wrong direction, and if we are reasonably intelligent we heed these signals, steer a different course, and come, finally, to the objective of our *definite chief aim*.

The author of this philosophy has devoted more than a quarter of a century to research for the purpose of discovering what characteristics were possessed and employed by the successful men and women in the field of business, industry, politics, statesmanship, religion, finance, transportation, literature, science, etc. This research has involved the reading of more than one thousand books of a scientific, business, and biographical nature, or an average of more than one such book a week.

One of the most startling discoveries made by this enormous amount of research was the fact that all the outstanding successes, regardless of the field of endeavor in which they were engaged, were people who met with reverses, adversity, temporary defeat, and in some instances actual *permanent failure* (as far as they, as individuals, were concerned). Not one single successful person was discovered whose success was attained without the experience of what, in many instances, seemed like unbearable obstacles that had to be mastered.

It was discovered also *that in exact ratio to the extent that these successful people met squarely and did not budge from defeat they arose to the heights of success.* In other words, success is measured, always, by the extent to which any individual meets and squarely deals with the obstacles that arise in the course of his procedure in pursuit of his *definite chief aim.*

Let us recall a few of the great successes of the world who met with temporary defeat, and some of whom were permanent failures, as far as they, as individuals, were concerned.

Columbus started out to find a shorter passage to India, but discovered America instead. He died a prisoner, in chains, a victim of the ignorance of his times.

Thomas A. Edison met with defeat after defeat, more than ten thousand unsuccessful efforts in all, before he made a revolving piece of wax record and reproduced the sound of the human voice. He met with similar defeat before he created the modern incandescent electric light bulb.

Alexander Graham Bell met with years of defeat before he perfected the long distance telephone.

Woolworth's first Five and Ten Cent Store project was not a success, and he had to master the most trying obstacles before he finally got his true bearings and rode high on the road to success.

Fulton's steamboat was a fizzle, and people laughed at him so hard that he had to sneak out at night and conduct his experiments privately.

The Wright brothers smashed many airplanes and suffered much defeat before they created a heavier-than-air flying machine that was practical.

Henry Ford almost starved to death, figuratively if not literally, before he successfully completed his first working model of an automobile. Nor was this the end of his troubles; he spent years perfecting the famous Model T car which made his fame and fortune.

Do not think, for one moment, that these men rode to success on the wings of plenty, without opposition of the most heart-rending nature. We are too apt to look at men in the hour of their triumph without taking into consideration the setbacks, defeats, and adversities through which they had to pass before success came.

Napoleon met with defeat after defeat before he made himself the great power that he was, and even then he finally met with permanent *failure*. At many times, it is recorded in his biographies, he contemplated committing suicide, so great were his disappointments.

The Panama Canal was not built without defeat. Time after time many of the deep cuts fell in and the engineers had to go back and do their work all over again. It looked, on many occasions, to those on the outside, at least, as if some of the heavy cuts never could be made to stand up. But perseverance, plus *a definite chief aim*, finally delivered to the world the most marvelous artificial body of water in the world, viewed from the standpoint of usefulness.

There comes to mind what this author believes to be the finest poem ever written on the subject of *failure*. It so thoroughly and clearly states the benefits of defeat that it is here reprinted, as follows;

WHEN NATURE WANTS A MAN!

(by Angela Morgan)

Copyright, 1926, by Dodd, Mead and Company, Inc.

When Nature wants to drill a man,
And thrill a man,
And skill a man.
When Nature wants to mold a man
To play the noblest part;
When she yearns with all her heart
To create so great and bold a man
That all the world shall praise—
Watch her method, watch her ways!

How she ruthlessly perfects
Whom she royally elects;
How she hammers him and hurts him,
And with mighty blows converts him
Into trial shapes of clay which only Nature understands—
While his tortured heart is crying and he lifts
    beseeching hands!—
How she bends but never breaks,
When his good she undertakes . . .
How she uses whom she chooses
And with every purpose infuses him,
By every art induces him
To try his splendor out—
Nature knows what she's about.

When Nature wants to take a man,
And shake a man,
And wake a man;
When Nature wants to make a man
To do the Future's will;
When she tries with all her skill
And she yearns with all her soul
To create him large and whole . . .
With what cunning she prepares him!
How she goads and never spares him,
How she whets him, and she frets him,
And in poverty begets him . . .

How she often disappoints

Whom she sacredly anoints,

With what wisdom she will hide him,

Never minding what betide him

Though his genius sob with slighting, and his pride may
    not forget!

Bids him struggle harder yet.

Makes him lonely

So that only

God's high messages shall reach him,

So that she may surely teach him

What the Hierarchy planned.

Though he may not understand

Gives him passions to command.

Now remorselessly she spurs him

With terrific ardor stirs him

When she poignantly prefers him!

When Nature wants to name a man

And fame a man

And tame a man;

When Nature wants to shame a man

To do his heavenly best . . .

When she tries the highest test

That the reckoning may bring—

When she wants a god or king!

How she reins him and restrains him

So his body scarce contains him
While she fires him
And inspires him!
Keeps him yearning, ever burning for a tantalizing goal—
Lures and lacerates his soul.
Sets a challenge for his spirit,
Draws it high when he's near it—
Makes a jungle that he clear it;
Makes a desert that he fear it
And subdue it if he can—
So doth Nature make a man.
Then, to test his spirit's wrath
Hurls a mountain in his path—
Puts a bitter choice before him
And relentless stands o'er him.
"Climb, or perish!" so she says . . .
Watch her purpose, watch her ways!

Nature's plan is wondrous kind
Could we understand her mind . . .
Fools are they who call her blind.
When his feet are tom and bleeding,
Yet his spirit mounts unheeding
All his higher powers speeding,
Blazing newer paths and fine;
When the force that is divine
Leaps to challenge every failure and his ardor still is sweet,

And love and hope are burning in the presence of
    defeat . . .
Lo, the crisis! Lo, the shout
That must call the leader out.
When the people need salvation
Doth he come to lead the nation . . .
Then doth Nature show her plan,
When the world has found—*a man!*

Do not be afraid of temporary defeat, but make sure
that you learn some lesson from every such defeat. That
which we call "experience" consists, largely, of what we
learn by mistakes—our own and those made by others—
but take care not to ignore the knowledge that may be
gained from mistakes.

LESSON FIFTEEN

Tolerance

Intolerance has caused more grief than any other of man's many forms of ignorance. Practically all wars grow out of intolerance. Misunderstandings between so-called "capital" and "labor" are usually the outgrowth of intolerance.

It is impossible for any man to observe the Law on *Accurate Thought*, without having first acquired the habit of tolerance, for the reason that intolerance causes a man to fold the Book of Knowledge and write "Finis, I know it all!" on the cover.

The most damaging form of intolerance grows out of religious and racial differences of opinion. Civilization, as we know it to-day, bears the deep wounds of gross intolerance all back down the ages, mostly those of a religious nature.

This is the most democratic country on earth. We are the most cosmopolitan people on earth. We are made up of all nationalities and people of every religious belief. We live side by side with neighbors whose religion differs from our own. Whether we are good neighbors or bad depends largely on how tolerant we are with one another.

Intolerance is the result of ignorance, or, stated conversely, the lack of *knowledge.* Well-informed men are seldom intolerant, because they know that no man knows enough to entitle him to judge others by his standards.

Through the principle of social heredity we inherit, from our environment, and through our early religious teachings, our ideas of religion. Our teachers themselves may not be always right, and if we bear this thought in mind, we would not allow such teachings to influence us to believe that we have a corner on *truth,* and that people whose teachings on this subject have been different from our own are all wrong.

There are many reasons why one should be tolerant, the chief of them being the fact that tolerance permits cool reason to guide one in the direction of *facts,* and this, in turn, leads to *accurate thinking.*

The man whose mind has been closed by intolerance, no matter of what brand or nature, can never become an *accurate thinker,* which is sufficient reason to cause us to master *intolerance.*

It may not be your *duty* to be tolerant with other people whose ideas, religious views, politics, and racial tendencies are different from yours, but it is *your privilege!* You do not have to ask permission of anyone to be tolerant; this is something that you control, in your own mind; therefore, the responsibility that goes with the choice is also your own.

Intolerance is closely related to the *six basic fears* described in the Law of *Self-Confidence,* and it may be stated as a positive fact that intolerance is always the result of either *fear* or *ignorance.* There are no exceptions to this rule. The moment another person (providing he, himself, is not intolerant) discovers that you are cursed with intolerance he can easily and quickly mark you as being either the victim of *fear* and *superstition* or what is worse, *ignorance!*

Intolerance closes the doorway to opportunity in a thousand ways, and shuts out the light of intelligence.

The moment you open your mind to *facts,* and take the attitude that the last word is seldom said on any subject—that there always remains the chance that still more truth may be learned on every subject, you begin to cultivate the Law of *Tolerance,* and if you practice this habit for long you will soon become a thinker, with ability to solve the problems that confront you in your struggle to make a place for yourself in your chosen field of endeavor.

LESSON SIXTEEN

Practicing the Golden Rule

This is, in some ways, the most important of the Seventeen Laws of Success. Despite the fact that the great philosophers for more than five thousand years back have all discovered the Law of the Golden Rule, and have made comment on it, the great majority of people of to-day look upon it as a sort of pretty text for preachers to build sermons on.

In truth the Golden Rule philosophy is based upon a powerful law which, when understood and faithfully practiced, will enable any man to get others to *co-operate* with him.

It is a well-known truth that most men follow the practice of returning good or evil, act for act. If you slander a man, he will slander you in return. If you praise a man, he will praise you in return. If you favor a man in business, he will favor you in return.

There are exceptions to this rule, to be sure, but by and large the law works out. Like attracts like. This is in accordance with a great natural law, and it works in every particle of matter and in every form of energy in the universe. Successful men attract successful men. Failures attract failures. The professional "bum" will make a bee line for the "flop" house, where he may associate with other "bums," even though he may be set down in a strange city, after dark.

The Law of the Golden Rule is closely related to the Law on *The Habit of Doing More than Paid For.* The very act of rendering more service than you are paid to render puts into operation this law through which "like attracts like," which is the selfsame law as that which forms the basis of the Golden Rule philosophy.

There is no escape from the fact that the man who renders more service than he is paid to render eventually will be eagerly sought by those who will be willing to pay him for more than he actually does. Compound interest on compound interest is Nature's rate, when she goes to pay the indebtedness incurred through application of this Law.

This law is so fundamental, so obvious, yet so simple. It is one of the great mysteries of human nature that

it is not more gener-
ally understood and
practiced. Back of
its use lie possibili-
ties that stagger the
imagination of the
most visionary per-
son. Through its use
may one learn the real

> Ideas are the most valuable products of the human mind. If you can create usable ideas and put them to work you can take whatever you wish for your pay.

secret—all the secret there is—about the art of *getting others to do that which we wish them to do.*

If you want a favor from someone, make it your business to seek out the person from whom you want the favor and, in an appropriate manner, render that person an equivalent of the favor you wish from him. If he does not respond at first, double the dose and render him another favor, and another, and another, and so on, until finally he will, out of shame if nothing more, come back and render you a favor.

You get others to co-operate with you by first co-operating with them!

The foregoing sentence is worth reading a hundred times, for it contains the gist of one of the most powerful laws available to the man who has the intention of attaining great success.

It may sometimes happen, and it will, that the particular individual to whom you render useful service will never respond and render you a similar service, but *keep this important truth in mind*—that even though one person fails to respond, someone else will observe the transaction and, out of a sportsman's desire to see justice done, or perhaps with a more selfish motive in mind, will render you the service to which you are entitled.

"Whatsoever a man soweth that shall he also reap!"

This is more than a mere preachment; it is a great practical truth that may be made the foundation of every successful achievement. From winding pathways or straight, every thought you send out, every deed you perform, will gather a flock of other thoughts or deeds according to its own nature, and come back home to you in due time.

There is no escape from this truth. It is as eternal as the universe, as sure of operation as the law of gravitation. To ignore it is to mark yourself as ignorant, or indifferent, either of which will destroy your chances of success.

The Golden Rule philosophy is the real basis on which children should be governed. It is also the real basis on which "children grown tall" should be managed. Through force, or by taking advantage of unfair circumstances, a man may build a fortune without observing the Golden Rule, and many do this, but such fortunes cannot bring happiness, because ill-gotten gain is bound to destroy the peace of mind of all who get it. Wealth created or acquired by the Golden Rule philosophy does not bring with it a flock of regrets, nor does it disturb the conscience and destroy the peace of mind.

Fortunate is the man who makes the Golden Rule his business or professional slogan and then lives up to the slogan faithfully, both literally and figuratively, observing the spirit of it as well as the letter.

The Habit of Health

We come now to the last of the seventeen factors of success. In previous chapters we have learned that success grows out of power; that power is organized knowledge expressed in definite action. No one can remain intensely active very long without good health. The mind will not function properly unless it has a sound body in which to function. Practically all of the other sixteen factors which enter into the building of success depend, for their successful application, upon a healthy body.

Good health is dependent, in the main, upon:

1. Proper food and air combinations
2. Proper elimination of waste fecal matter
3. Proper exercise
4. Right thinking

It is not the purpose of this chapter to present a treatise on how to remain healthy, as that is a task which belongs to the specialists in physical and mental therapeutics. However, no harm can be done by calling attention to the fact that poor health is usually superinduced by poor elimination. People who live in cities and eat the artificially prepared foods will find it necessary to constantly aid nature in the eliminative processes by flushing the intestinal tract with water at regular intervals of not more than one week each. Practically all headaches, sluggishness, loss of "pep" and similar feelings are mostly due to auto-intoxication, or intestinal poisoning through improper elimination.

Most people eat too much. Such people will find it helpful if they go on a ten-day fast about three times a year, during which time they refrain from taking food of any nature whatsoever. During a fast the intestinal tract should be flushed with water daily. The experience of fasting will bring to all who have never tried it health-building values which can be attained in no other way. No one should experiment with fasting, dieting, or any other form of self-administered therapeutics, except under the direction of a physician of experience in such matters.

Sex Energy a Health Builder

As a closing thought for this chapter the author has chosen to inject a very brief statement concerning the therapeutic value of sex energy. The foundation of fact which justifies the reference to sex, as a health builder, will be laid in the following manner:

It is a well-known fact that *thought* is the most powerful energy available to man.

It is equally as well known that negative thoughts of worry and envy and hatred and fear will destroy the digestive processes and bring about illness; this by reason of the fact that negative thought inhibits the flow of certain glandular contents which are essential in the digestive processes.

Negative thoughts cause "short circuits" in the nerve lines which carry nervous energy (or life force) from the central distributing station, the brain, to all parts of the body, where this energy performs its natural task of nourishment and of removal of worn-out cells and waste matter.

Sex energy is a highly vitalizing, positive force, when it is in a state of agitation, during the period of sexual contact, and because it is powerful it sweeps over the entire nervous system of the body and unties any "short circuits" which may exist in any of the nerve lines, thus insuring a complete flow of nervous energy to *all* parts of the body.

Sexual emotion is the most powerful of all the human emotions, and when it is actively engaged, it reaches and vitalizes every cell in every organ of the body, thereby causing the organs to function in a normal manner. Total abstinence, sexually, was not one of Nature's plans, and those who do not understand this truth usually pay for their ignorance out of a trust fund which Nature provided for the maintenance of health.

Thought controls all voluntary movements of the body. Are we in accord on this statement? Very well, if thought controls all voluntary movements of the body, may it not also be made to control, of at least materially influence, all involuntary movements of the body?

Thoughts of a negative nature, such as fear, worry, and anxiety, not only inhibit the flow of the digestive juices, but they also "tie knots" in the nerve lines which carry nervous energy to the various organs of the body

Thoughts of a *positive* nature untie these knots in the nerve lines and permit the nervous energy to pass through. *Sex emotion is the most powerful form of positive thought.* Sex energy is Nature's own "medicine," proof of which is obvious if one will observe the state of mind and the perfectly relaxed condition of the body, following sexual contact.

Brief as it is, the foregoing statement should be made the starting point for some intelligent analysis of this subject by the reader of this book. Let us be open minded on this subject of sex. No one knows the last word in connection with the subject; most of us do not even know the first word. Therefore, let us not pass judg-

ment on a subject concerning which we know so very little until we have at least done some intelligent thinking
on the subject. For all that most of us know, both poverty and ill health may be mastered through a complete
understanding of the subject of sex energy, and this for
the reason that sex energy is the most powerful mind
stimulant known.

The Thirty
Most Common
Causes of Failure

Through the foregoing pages you have had a brief description of the seventeen factors through which success is attained. Now let us turn our attention to some of the factors which cause failure. Check the list and you will perhaps find here the cause of any failure, or temporary defeat, which you may have experienced. The list is based upon accurate analysis of over twenty thousand failures, and it covers men and women in every calling,

1. *Unfavorable hereditary foundation* (This cause of failure stands at the head of the list. Bad breeding is a handicap against which there is but little remedy, and it is one for which the individual, unfortunately, is not responsible.)

2. Lack of a well-defined purpose, or definite major aim toward which to strive.

3. Lack of ambition to aim above mediocrity

4. Insufficient education

5. Lack of self-discipline and tact, generally manifesting itself through all sorts of excesses; especially in sexual desires and eating

6. Ill health, usually due to preventable causes

7. Unfavorable environment during childhood, when character was being formed, resulting in vicious habits of body and mind

8. Procrastination

9. Lack of persistence and courage to blame one's self with one's failures

10. Negative personality

11. Lack of well-defined sexual urge

12. An uncontrollable desire to get *something* for *nothing* usually manifesting itself in habits of gambling

13. Lack of decision

14. One or more of the six basic fears described elsewhere in this book

15. Poor selection of a mate in marriage

16. Overcaution, destroying initiative and self-confidence

17. Poor selection of associates in business

18. Superstition and prejudice, generally traceable to lack of knowledge of natural laws

19. Wrong selection of occupation

20. Dissipation of energies, through lack of understanding of the law of concentration, resulting in what is commonly known as "jack-of-all-trades"

21. Lack of thrift

22. Lack of enthusiasm

23. Intolerance

24. Intemperance in eating, drinking, and sexual activities

25. Inability to co-operate with others in a spirit of harmony

26. Possession of power which was not acquired through self-effort, by slow, evolutionary processes of experience (as in the case of one who inherits wealth, or is placed in a position of power to which he is not entitled on merit)

27. Dishonesty

28. Egotism and vanity

29. Guessing instead of thinking

30. Lack of capital

Some may wonder why "lack of capital" was placed at the bottom of the list, and the answer is that anyone who can qualify with a reasonably high grade, on the other twenty-nine causes of failure, can always get all the capital needed for any purpose whatsoever.

The foregoing list does not include all the causes of failure, but it does represent the most common causes. Some may object that "unfavorable luck" should have been added to the list, but the answer to this complaint is that luck, or the law of chance, is subject to mastery by all who understand how to apply the seventeen factors of success. However, in fairness to those who may never have had the opportunity to master the seventeen factors of success, it must be admitted that luck, or an unfavorable turn of the wheel of chance, is sometimes the cause of failure.

Those who are inclined to attribute all their failures to "circumstances" or luck, should remember the blunt injunction laid down by Napoleon, who said, "To hell with circumstances! I create circumstances." Most "circumstances" and unfavorable results of luck are self-made, also. *Let us not forget this!*

Here is a statement of fact, and a confession, that is well-worth remembering. *The law of success philosophy, which is now rendering useful service to men and women all over this earth, is very largely the result of nearly twenty years of so-called failure upon the part of the author.* In the more extensive course on the Law of Success philosophy, under the lesson on "Profiting by Failure," the student will observe that the author met with failure and adversity and reverses so often that he might have been justified in crying out, "Luck is against me!" Seven major failures, and more scores of minor failures than the author can, or cares to remember, laid the foundation for a philosophy which is now bringing success to tens of thousands of people, *including the author!* "Bad luck" has been harnessed and put to work, and the whole world is now paying substantial monetary tribute to the man who ferreted out the happy thought that even luck can be changed, and failures can be capitalized.

> "There is a wheel on which the affairs of men revolve, and its mechanism is such that it prevents any man from being always fortunate."

True enough! There is such a wheel of life, but it is rotating continuously. If this wheel brings misfortune to-day, it can be made to bring good fortune to-morrow. If this were not true, the Law of Success philosophy would be a farce and a fake, offering nothing but false hope.

The author was once told that he would always be a failure because he was born under an unfavorable star! Something must have happened to antidote the bad influence of that star, and something *has happened*. That "something" is the power to master obstacles by first mastering self, which grew out of understanding and application of the Law of Success philosophy. If the seventeen factors of success can offset the bad influence of a star for this author, they can do the same for *you*, or for any other person.

Laying our misfortunes to the influence of stars is just another way of acknowledging our ignorance or our laziness. The only place that stars can bring you bad luck is in your own mind. You have possession of that mind, and it has the power to master all the bad influences which stand between you and success, including that of the stars.

If you really wish to see the cause of your bad luck and misfortunes, do not look up toward the stars; look in a mirror! You are the master of your fate! You are the captain of your soul. And this by reason of the fact that you have a mind which you, alone, control, and this mind can be stimulated and made to form a direct contact with all the power you need to solve any problem that may confront you. The person who blames his troubles upon stars thereby challenges the existence of Infinite Intelligence, or God, if you prefer that name.

The Mystery of the Power of Thought!

In front of the author's study, at Broadway and Forty-fourth Street, in New York City, stands the Paramount Building; a great tall, impressive building which serves as a daily reminder of the great power of *thought.*

Come, stand with me by the window of my study and let us analyze this modern skyscraper. Tell me, if you can, of what materials the building is constructed. Immediately you will say, "Why, it is built of brick and steel girders and plate glass and lumber," and you will be partly right, but you have not told the entire story.

The brick and steel and other materials which went into the *physical* portion of the building were necessary, but before any of those materials were laid into place the building, in its entirety, was constructed of another sort of material. It was first built, in the mind of Adolph Zukor, out of the intangible stuff known as *thought*.

Everything you have or ever will have, good or bad, was attracted to you by the nature of your *thoughts*. Positive thoughts attract positive, desirable objects; negative thoughts attract poverty and misery and a flock of other sorts of undesirable objects. Your brain is the magnet to which everything you possess clings, and make no mistake about this, your brain will not attract success while you are thinking of poverty and failure.

Every man is where he is, as the result of his own dominating thoughts, just as surely as night follows day. *Thought* is the only thing that you absolutely control, a statement of fact which we repeat because of its great significance. You do not control, entirely, the money you possess, or the love and friendship that you enjoy; you had nothing to do with your coming into the world and you will have but little to do with the time of your going; but you do have *everything* to do with the state of your own mind. You can make that mind positive or you can permit it to become *negative,* as the result of outside influences and suggestions. Divine Providence gave you supreme control of your own mind, and with this control the responsibility that is now yours to make the best use of it.

In your own mind you can fashion a great building, similar to the one which stands in front of the author's study, and then transform that mental picture into a reality, just as Adolph Zukor did, because the material out of which he constructed the Paramount Building is available to every human being; moreover, it is *free*. All you have to do is to appropriate it and put it to your use. This universal material, as we have said, is the *power of thought*.

The difference between success and failure is largely a matter of the difference between positive and negative thought. A negative mind will not attract a fortune. Like attracts like. Nothing attracts success as quickly as success. Poverty begets more poverty. Become successful and the whole world will lay its treasures at your feet and want to do something to help you become more successful. Show signs of poverty and the entire world will try to take away that which you have of value. You can borrow money at the bank when you are prosperous and do not need it, but try and arrange a loan when you are poverty-stricken, or when some great emergency faces you. You are the master of your own destiny because you control the one thing which can change and redirect the course of human destinies, the power of *thought*. Let this great truth sink into your consciousness and this book will have marked the most important turning point of your life.

How to Convert This Philosophy into Cash

The author is engaged in the business of helping other people to find themselves. His work consists of two forms of procedure, as follows: First, the student is taught how to co-ordinate and apply the seventeen factors of the Law of Success philosophy in the solution of any problem. Second, the student is analyzed and a chart is made of his or her good qualities and poor ones. In other words the student's entire mental equipment is thoroughly diagnosed and the result plainly stated in a written chart, which shows what line of work should be followed and the best plan for carrying out that work. Whenever possible the author interviews the student in person. When this is not possible the student is served through class instruction, or by correspondence, if he lives at a great distance from New York City.

The Nature of Personal Interviews

Personal interviews between students of the Law of Success philosophy and the author are for the purpose of aiding the student in applying this philosophy to the end that his or her *definite chief aim* may be selected, and a practical working plan for its achievement adopted. The interview constitutes a very effective application of the Master Mind principle, through which two minds are co-ordinated for the purpose of attaining a given objective.

These interviews are productive of phenomena which often startle both the author and his students. For illustration, not long ago a lady called for an interview for the purpose of finding the life work for which she was best fitted. She had been a student of the Law of Success philosophy for several months, and had mastered the eight textbooks on the subject, and was familiar with the fundamentals of this philosophy. Within fifteen minutes after her arrival at the author's office she had "stepped up" the vibrations of her mind to where she was "tuning in" on the Master Mind principle. The creative faculty of her imagination began to work rapidly, with the result that the ideas described below began to "flash" into her mind.

The author made notes of these ideas, which came as fast as he could write in shorthand. The flow of ideas did not cease, but was voluntarily cut off because the time of her interview had expired and another client was waiting. The ideas are listed here, just as she received them.

Forty Unique Ideas
for Making Money

⟡

Interpreted by Miss M. C. through the Aid of the Master Mind Principle

1. Rewrite the Law of Success philosophy in a brief form which can be presented in one volume, at a very low cost, so it can be placed in the hands of hundreds of thousands of students who might otherwise never have the benefit of such a philosophy of success, and permit teachers of the philosophy, throughout the world, to use this book as a textbook, in private classes and success clubs to be organized by them. (Author's note: The book you hold in your hands is the concrete result of the foregoing idea.)

2. A chain of automatic gas filling stations at which the motorist may serve himself, day or night, by dropping coins in a slot machine.

3. A chain of automatic news stands, dispensing magazines, newspapers and periodicals through slot machines.

4. A chain of automatic five and ten cent stores, dispensing merchandise through slot machines, thus saving labor and loss from stealage over the counters.

5. An elastic support, to be made of flexible steel, which will cause one to hold the spine and shoulders erect, thereby permitting the nervous energy to pass freely to all parts of the body.

6. A vibrating machine, to be attached to the seats of chairs of office and factory workers who must work in a sitting position, which may be turned on at intervals during working hours, for the purpose of distributing the nervous energy and preventing fatigue, or "laziness."

7. New profession of Environment Artist, whose work will be that of creating a positive environment in home, office or workshop, store, etc., for the purpose of relieving the monotony of such places.

8. Combination locks for automobiles (keyless locks) for the prevention of theft, joy riding, etc.

9. A new profession to be known as "Personality Artist," whose members will assist men and women in the selection of clothes of appropriate lines and color harmony, to work in conjunction with high-grade

clothing stores, and whose services will be free to the customer.

10. Research Secretary, whose business it will be to gather and classify data on any subject.

11. Country Club for people of small means, equipped with playgrounds for children, and competent nurses and play directors who will assume full responsibility for children during certain hours of the day or night, to be conducted in connection with suburban real estate developments, as an added inducement for people to locate there.

12. Idea Specialist for daily newspapers whose business it would be to create new and unique ideas for sales and advertising campaigns for small merchants who cannot afford to employ expensive people, and whose services would be free to all advertisers of the paper.

13. A Summer Camp Ground, near the city, where people may secure a plot of ground large enough for a tent, or small portable buildings, and sufficient ground for a garden, on a rental basis within the means of the man of small income.

14. Week-end outing information, supplying data on all near-by places of interest where the motorists may spend a day's or a weekend's outing, with road maps, descriptive literature etc., to be operated by chain of filling stations as a means of building up their business.

15. A moving picture service operated for the purpose of making short reels of children at play (to preserve the memory of their childhood days for parents), birthday parties, weddings,business gatherings, and banquets.

16. Typewriters for rent in hotels and on Pullman cars, through the aid of coin slot machines.

17. Box lunches for office and factory workers, made up of home-cooked foods, consisting of a properly balanced diet of pure food products. (Business can be conducted by a housewife, from her own kitchen.) Several clients of the author are now profitably employing this idea.

18. Home baking of pies, bread, and cakes, selling the output through regular arrangement with a number of local grocers and drug stores.

19. Book giving accurate information to beginners in the field of writing, as to subjects on which to write, and where and how to market their manuscripts.

20. Summer house boat that can be propelled by an automobile, for rent to motorists who wish to spend a part of their time on water and at the same time have their motor cars available for land use.

21. Window card advertising service for retail stores, carrying snappy, interesting epigrams instead of news pictures, that will cause the crowd to stop and read.

22. A set of fifty-two blotters, to be used for advertising purposes, each blotter carrying an epigram or

motto appropriate to the business of the advertiser using the blotter, one blotter to be mailed out to a selected mailing list each week. (This is a plan to enable a printer to build up a business on printed blotters.)

23. Fountain drinks made of the juices of vegetables which have food value, and served fresh each day, without preservatives or chemicals of any sort.

24. Signs for office doors made of removable glass, which may be taken along when a tenant moves.

25. A Clearings House for the exchange of practical sales ideas among retailers.

26. A home nursery, to be conducted by married women who wish an independent source of income, to serve women who wish to leave their children in reliable hands.

27. Clothing Exchange, where used clothes may be exchanged for other used clothes.

28. New York City mailing address for out of the city small firms and individuals who wish their mail sent to New York and then forwarded, because of the prestige of the New York address, on a service fee basis of five dollars per month for each client. (Two hundred such clients would give one person a very substantial income.)

29. Moving pictures for children only, catering exclusively to the child mind, based upon plots which edu-

cate as well as entertain, to be distributed through the public schools.

30. Comic strip for newspapers, advertising some brand of merchandise, and at the same time entertaining, to be run in local newspapers by merchants selling the product advertised.

31. Success Editor for newspapers, to conduct a daily column based upon the material in the eight volumes of the Law of Success, through a working alliance with the author of the Law of Success.

32. Removable feet for hosiery, made of an absorbent material which will keep the feet free from perspiration, thus adding to the life of the hosiery and the health and comfort of the wearer.

33. Reversible neck ties, made of two sorts of material, thus giving the service of two different ties.

34. Special sets for men, consisting of shirt, tie, hose, and handkerchief to match, to be packed in a neat box, and sold at popular prices.

35. Elastic band fastened to top of trousers (on inside) thus eliminating the necessity of belt or suspenders.

36. Daily menu made up of health foods, to be syndicated in newspapers.

37. Physical Culture Club where exercise is given through properly designed dances, thus making physical exercise a pleasure instead of a torture.

38. A Sales Service Agency, to be conducted by telephone, providing real estate dealers, automobile dealers, or any other business, with properly qualified prospective purchasers. (This plan may be conducted in any city, and it has unlimited possibilities for the person who understands how to present a telephone preliminary sales talk.)

39. House organs for small business firms, to be printed on the mimeograph, at a cost much less than that of printing, in small quantities. (Note: This idea has been put into use by two young men in New York City, and they are prepared to supply all the copy and other material necessary for others who wish to carry on a similar business in other cities. They have copy suitable for practically all sorts of business, such as banks, life insurance, real estate, retail stores, etc. Their names will be supplied to interested persons upon application to the author of this book.)

40. Organize Success Classes in business houses for the purpose of teaching the employees how to apply the Law of Success philosophy in their respective positions, to the end that both they and their employers may profit. (Note: This idea is now being carried out. It will provide employment for thousands of men and women who will prepare themselves to teach the Law of Success philosophy.)

Think of the possibilities of stupendous achievement, financial and otherwise, with a mind that can create forty unique money-making ideas in less than ten minutes. Such a mind has no limitations. The Law of Success philosophy was organized for the purpose of "stepping up" any mind and causing it to make use of its potential powers. Reports from students of this philosophy from all over the world show that they are experiencing results similar to those described in this book.

The foregoing are but a few of the many hundreds of useful ideas which develop from application of the Master Mind principle, in the author's daily contact with his students who come for personal interviews in connection with their sundry problems of life. These interviews turn an interesting side light on human nature, as they are connected with practically every human problem, ranging all the way from the man who wishes to improve the appearance and habits of his 1898 model wife without hurting her pride, to the man who wishes to find a way to increase his earning capacity by a few thousands of dollars per year. Such a great variety of discussion brings knowledge of the man animal which could be secured in no other way. When men and women come to the author and pay him a substantial sum to listen to their troubles and to offer plans for solving their problems, they do not make any attempt to deceive, nor do they try to set their best foot forward for the sake of making a favorable impression. They discuss their weaknesses as readily as they do their virtues.

In the solution of the problems of his clients, the author often finds it necessary to bring different clients together in business and professional alliances. One man will have a useful invention, or an idea for the expansion of some business enterprise, but lacks the capital to promote it. Perhaps the very next client will have ability to raise capital. The two are brought together and shown how to pool their resources through the aid of the Master Mind principle.

There is a practical solution for every human problem. When two or more people sit down and seriously concentrate their minds upon the solution of any problem, in a spirit of harmonious co-operation, ways and means leading to the desired end suggest themselves in a most miraculous fashion.

Not all students of the Law of Success philosophy have the opportunity to come to the author for personal interviews, as thousands of them live outside of the United States. These students receive help from the author through the aid of a Personal Analysis Questionnaire. This Questionnaire brings to the author a perfect mental picture of the one who fills it out, and thus provides the necessary data out of which the solution of practically any problem may be evolved without the author seeing the student.

The author is preparing to establish an authorized analyst and teacher in every city in the United States and eventually in many cities in other

> If you must slander someone do not speak it, but write it—write it in the sand, near the water's edge.

countries, who will personally teach the Law of Success philosophy and serve students of the philosophy through personal interviews, just as the author is doing here in New York City. Undoubtedly many of these teachers will be recruited from the rapidly declining profession of the clergy, as these splendid gentlemen have the personality and the education and the intelligence and the knowledge of pedagogy and the understanding of human problems which are so essential in the successful interpretation of the Law of Success philosophy.

Other teachers will be recruited from the business and professional fields. The philosophy will be taught in every language spoken in the civilized world, which calls for teachers and analysts of every nationality. The necessary steps to be taken by those who wish to become teachers and analysts will be thoroughly explained by the author of the Law of Success, upon application addressed to his New York City office.

A Message to Those Who Have Tried and Failed!

The author would not be satisfied to send this book out on its mission of inspirational service without adding this short chapter as a personal message to those who have tried and "failed!"

Failure! What a misunderstood word! What chaos and distress and poverty and heartaches have come out of misinterpretation of this word.

Just a few days ago the author stood on a humble spot of ground in the mountains of Kentucky, not far from his own birthplace, where a well-known "failure" was born. When a very young man this "failure" went away to war, commissioned as a captain.

His record was so poor that he was demoted to corporal and finally returned home as a private.

He took up surveying, but he could not make a living at this work and very soon he was humiliated by having his instruments sold for his debts.

Next he took up law, but he got very few cases, and most of these he lost on account of incompetence.

He became engaged to a young lady, but changed his mind and failed to show up for the wedding.

He drifted into politics and by chance was elected to Congress, but his record was so drab that it caused no favorable comment. Everything he undertook brought him humiliation and failure.

Then a miracle happened! A great love experience came into his life, and despite the fact that the girl who aroused this love passed beyond the Great Divide, the lingering thoughts of that love caused this "Nobody" to fight his way out of his humble role as failure, and at the age of fifty-two he became the greatest and most beloved President who ever occupied the White House.

Men are made, or broken, according to the use they make of the *power* of thought. Failure may be transformed into success overnight, when one becomes inspired with a great impelling motive to succeed. The eight basic motives which move men to action have been described in a previous chapter. One of these eight is the motive of *love*.

Abraham Lincoln's love for Anne Rutledge turned mediocrity into greatness. He found himself through the sorrow that came to him through her death.

Elbert Hubbard left his impress for good upon the world, through the expression of genius that was inspired by Alice Hubbard, his second wife.

Henry Ford is the richest and most powerful man now living. He had to master poverty, illiteracy, and other handicaps which the average man never encounters. He became successful because of the love inspired by a truly great woman, his wife, and this despite the fact that his biographers have never mentioned her name.

Every Ford automobile, and the Ford millions, and every Ford factory, and all that Henry Ford has accomplished for the good of mankind, may be appropriately submitted as evidence of the soundness of the Law of Success philosophy, as he is the most practical student of this philosophy now living. From his life work, more than from any other source, has come the material that made this philosophy a reality.

The seed of all success lies sleeping in well-defined *motive!*

Without a *burning desire* to achieve, superinduced by one or more of the eight basic *motives*, no man ever becomes a genius.

Motivated by a highly developed urge of sex, Napoleon became the greatest leader of men of his time. His ignoble ending was the result of his lack of observance of two of the seventeen factors of success, namely, Self-Control and the Golden Rule.

Lester Park entered the moving picture business twenty-five years ago, at about the same time that the author began the organization of the Law of Success philosophy. The "miracle" which transformed Mr. Park from a self-styled "failure" into an outstanding success was described in a page editorial written by the author and published recently in a New York newspaper. This editorial is here reproduced as a fitting close for this chapter:

"Another Miracle

"For twenty-five years I have been studying, measuring, and analyzing human beings. My research has brought me in contact with over twenty thousand men and women. Two people out of this vast army stand out in bold contrast with nearly all the others. These two are Henry Ford and Lester Park.

"Mr. Ford's general average, according to my last analysis, was ninety-five per cent. Lester Park's general average, according to an analysis which I have just completed for him, is ninety-four per cent. I first analyzed Henry Ford over twenty-three years ago.

At that time his rating, on the seventeen factors of success, was sixty-seven per cent. His gradual rise from sixty-seven per cent to ninety-five per cent has been an outstanding achievement, but nothing to compare with the transformation which took place in Lester Park's mental machinery, over a period of but a few weeks, as shown by the accompanying graphic chart of his analysis.

"When I first analyzed Mr. Park (as indicated by the dotted line, at the bottom of the chart), his general average was forty-five per cent. Less than a month later I made a second analysis and lo! he had jumped from "zero" to one hundred per cent an two of the most important of the seventeen factors of success, and had made astounding advances on many of the other factors.

"A Sweeping Endorsement

"This analysis chart, showing Lester Park's two ratings on the factors which give men power and wealth, is a sweeping endorsement of the belief which many philosophers have held, that *all success is merely a state of mind!* That man is lifted to great heights of power, or dashed into oblivion, solely by the thoughts he releases, on the wings of the ether.

"Solitary Confinement

"Lester Park was formerly one of the most active moving picture executives in America. His name was linked with those of other men who have since made huge fortunes out of this business many believe to be still in its infancy). But something "snapped" in Lester Park's mental machinery. He lost his grip on himself. His self-confidence dropped to zero. He ceased to have a definite chief aim. He drew himself away from contact with others in his profession, thereby depriving himself of the greatest of all the Laws of Success, the Master Mind. (A mind that is a composite of two or more minds working in perfect harmony, for the attainment of some definite objective.)

For years Lester Park committed himself, figuratively and literally, to solitary confinement, in a dark dungeon! *That dungeon was his own mind and he, himself, carried the key to the door.*

"The Wheel of Fate

"In September, 1928, I conducted a class on the Laws of Success, at the Waldorf-Astoria Hotel, in New York City. By a queer turn of the wheel of chance—or was it the "wheel of fate"?—Lester Park became a student in that class. The transformation which has taken place in Lester Park occurred in a fractional part of a minute, during the first half hour of my first lecture! In a single sentence I made a statement which served as a key that unlocked the door to the cell in which Lester Park had confined himself, and *he stepped out, ready to pick up the reins where he had laid them down several years ago.* The transformation is no imaginary one. It has been both real and complete. Within two weeks' time after the light again shone into the brain of Lester Park he had completed all arrangements for the production of one of the greatest pictures of his career. When I say he had 'completed all arrangements' I mean just that! The money for the production was offered him from more than one source. Friends whom he had known in the heydey of his career as a producer suddenly appeared upon the scene as if by magic, and greeted him like long-lost brothers! 'Corianton,' the dream picture of his life, became a living, pulsating reality, and that picture is now in preparation for production.

"A Modern Miracle Had Happened!

"That miracle brings great joy to my heart, because it proves, once more, that the child of my heart and brain—*the Law of Success philosophy*—is destined to emancipate millions of Lester Parks from the dark dungeons of despair to which they have confined themselves. Over twenty years ago Andrew Carnegie gave me an idea which caused me to start a period of labor and research that has lasted almost a quarter of a century. That idea was the hub around which the Law of Success philosophy has been built. I have lived to see it bring freedom to no less than ten thousand people, and to how many more it has brought similar freedom I have no way of knowing, because the philosophy is now being studied by thousands of students in nearly every civilized country on earth, with whom I have not personally come in contact.

"A Prophecy Fulfilled

"Years ago, when I predicted that Henry Ford would one day become the most powerful man on earth, my statement caused me great embarrassment, because Ford had not then shown any signs of becoming the world's richest man. I stood back of that prediction and lived to see it become more than justified.

"Another Prophecy

"I now publicly predict that Lester Park will become the most successful moving picture producer in the field. I have the best of reasons to believe—even to

know—that this prophecy is well on the road toward fulfillment, and I shall be willing to assume full responsibility for it.

"The scientific world is on the border of the greatest of all discoveries, and when the nature of this discovery has been announced it will over-shadow all else that mankind has learned about the physical laws of nature and things material. The nature of this discovery was discussed with this writer by the late Dr. Alexander Graham Bell and Dr. Elmer R. Gates, nineteen years ago, but the principle to which I refer was not then sufficiently understood to enable man to harness and use it. Nineteen years of experimentation have changed this, and the world is now practically in possession of knowledge of a law which will enable any man to change the course of his worldly destiny at will!

"Study the graphic chart analysis of Lester Park and you may gather a slight idea of what man may do for himself when he has learned how to harmonize himself with natural laws.

"Napoleon Hill."

"Editor's Note—

"The above statement is made under the personal signature of Napoleon Hill, author of the Law of Success philosophy. Those who do not know of Mr. Hill or his work are entitled to know that he has been engaged, for almost a quarter of a century, in experimenting with the human mind. In his research he has had valuable assistance from the best-known scientists of the world, such men as the late Dr. Alexander Graham Bell, Dr. Elmer R. Gates, Chas. P. Steinmetz, and Luther Burbank. In a recent series of articles which appeared in *McClure's Magazine,* Henry Ford publicly admitted that the philosophy outlined in Mr. Hill's Seventeen Laws of Success had been the foundation of his own rise to power and wealth.

"Mr. Hill is the Success Editor of the *New York Evening Graphic,* and his 'Success Column' is appearing in other newspapers. Through this column he has kindled anew the fires of enthusiasm and ambition in the minds of thousands of men and women who had all but lost hope of achieving financial success.

"The late Elbert H. Gary, former Chairman of the Board of the United States Steel Corporation, was preparing, at the time of his death, to present the Law of Success course to every employee of the steel corporation who could read

English, at a total cost of something like one hundred and fifty thousand dollars.

"Cyrus H. K. Curtis, owner, of the *Saturday Evening Post*, and one of the most successful publishers of the world, openly endorsed Mr. Hill's discoveries and asked permission to reprint material from one of the lessons, in the *Philadelphia Public Ledger*.

"Wm. Howard Taft, former President of the United States, endorsed the Law of Success philosophy in a most enthusiastic letter which Mr. Hill received from him.

"Edwin C. Barnes, a business associate of Thomas A. Edison, not only endorsed the Law of Success philosophy, and gave it credit for enabling him to retire from business, with all the wealth he wants, at the age of forty-five, but also gave a most sweeping endorsement of Mr. Hill personally, whom he has known for twenty years.

"From this it may be said, without exaggeration, that Napoleon Hill is one of the great thinkers of the age—because no man could possibly command the respect and secure the endorsement of such men as those who have endorsed him, unless he were a sound thinker."

This Is an Age of Action!

Summarizing the, seventeen factors of success described in this volume, the reader may better grasp the entire philosophy by keeping in mind the fact that success is based upon *power;* that power is knowledge expressed in *action*.

All of the major stimuli which arouse the mind and put it into action have been described in this volume. The main purpose of the seventeen factors of success is that of providing one with practical plans and methods of application for the use of these stimuli.

Careful analysis has disclosed the startling fact that a single incident, or experience, often results in such marked influence upon a mind of the most mediocre type that the owner of that mind surpasses, in achievement, others who have superior and better trained minds.

The Law of Success, as described through the seventeen factors (outlined in this volume, provides all the known methods of mind stimulation which inspire the individual with high ambition and supply the courage essential for the attainment of the object of that ambition.

It is hardly sufficient to say that one may achieve more if one will undertake more. The author has aimed to offer the individual a practical mind stimulant, or source of inspiration, which may be used to build greater ambition and supply the motive for *action* in carrying out that ambition.

Ninety-five per cent of the energy of the human mind remains passive throughout life. The major purpose of this philosophy of success is to supply the stimuli which will arouse this sleeping ninety-five per cent of mind energy and put it to work. How? By planting in the mind some strong motive that will lead to action. By stepping up the mind, through contact with other minds, and causing it to vibrate on a higher plane.

This volume inadequately describes the majority of the seventeen factors of success. The more extensive outline of the philosophy, in eight volumes, devotes as much space to each of the other sixteen factors of success as is here devoted to the Master Mind.

In the more extensive volumes the subjects of Accurate Thought and Enthusiasm have been so thoroughly discussed that the exact method of mind stimulation has been made plain. The author regrets that the limitations of this volume made impossible a more thorough description of the exact procedure in applying the known sources of mind stimuli.

Readers who desire more detailed data concerning the Law of Success philosophy, or who wish to ask questions regarding methods of applying the philosophy in connection with their own problems, have the privilege of addressing the author for this purpose. If more personal service is desired than that which can be supplied through correspondence, the reader should make application to the nearest teacher of the Law of Success philosophy, names and addresses of whom will be supplied upon request.

To the extent that available time will permit, the author will gladly assist any reader of this book to properly interpret and make practical use of this philosophy.

> The man who sows a single beautiful thought in the mind of another renders the world, through that act, a greater service than that rendered by all the fault-finders combined.